AFRICAN STUDIES
HISTORY, POLITICS, ECONOMICS, AND CULTURE

Edited by
Molefi Asante
Temple University

A ROUTLEDGE SERIES

African Studies
History, Politics, Economics, and Culture

Molefi Asante, *General Editor*

LAW, MORALITY AND INTERNATIONAL ARMED INTERVENTION
The United Nations and ECOWAS in Liberia

Mourtada Déme

Foreword by
Robert Jackson

Routledge
New York & London

Published in 2005 by
Routledge
Taylor & Francis Group
711 Third Avenue
New York, NY 10017

Published in Great Britain by
Routledge
Taylor & Francis Group
2 Park Square
Milton Park, Abingdon
Oxon OX14 4RN

First issued in paperback 2013

International Standard Book Number-10: 0-415-97595-6 (Hardcover)
International Standard Book Number-13: 978-0-415-97595-7 (Hardcover)
International Standard Book Number-13: 978-0-415-65539-2 (Paperback)

Library of Congress Card Number 2005014503

Library of Congress Cataloging-In-Publication Data

Déme, Mourtada.
   Law, morality and international armed intervention : the United Nations and ECOWAS in Liberia / by Mourtada Déme.
         p. cm. -- (African studies)
   Includes bibliographical references and index.
   ISBN 0-415-97595-6
   1. Liberia--History--Civil War, 1989---Participation, Foreign. 2. Liberia--History--Civil War, 1989---Participation, African. 3. United Nations--Liberia. 4. Economic Community of West African States. 5. Africa, West--Politics and government--1960- I. Title. II. African studies (Routledge (Firm))
   DT636.5.D46 2005
   341.23'6662'09049--dc22   2005014503

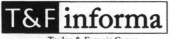

Taylor & Francis Group
is the Academic Division of T&F Informa plc.

Visit the Taylor & Francis Web site at
http://www.taylorandfrancis.com

and the Routledge Web site at
http://www.routledge-ny.com

To the memory of Mame Ndiack Déme.
For my parents.

Contents

List of Abbreviations

AAFC	Allied Armed Forces of the Community
ADF	Allied Democratic Forces
AFL	Armed Forces of Liberia
AJIL	American Journal of International Law
CEAO	Communauté Economique de l'Afrique de l'Ouest
ECOMOG	ECOWAS Cease-fire Monitoring Group
ECOWAS	Economic Community of West African States
ICISS	International Commission on Intervention and State Sovereignty
ICJ	International Court of Justice
IFI	International Financial Institutions
IGNU	Interim Government of National Unity
IMF	International Monetary Fund
INFPL	Independent National Patriotic Front of Liberia
INN	International Negotiation Network
LNTG	Liberian National Transitional Government
LPC	Liberian Peace Council
LURD	Liberian United for Reconciliation and Democracy
MSC	Mediation and Security Council
NAM	Non-Aligned Movement
NATO	North Atlantic Treaty Organization
NGO	Non-Governmental Organization
NPRAG	National Patriotic Reconstruction Assembly Government

NPFL	National Patriotic Front of Liberia
OAU	Organization of African Unity
SMC	Standing Mediation Committee
TLA	Transitional Legislative Assembly
UEMOA	Union Economique et Monétaire Ouest Africaine
ULIMO	United Liberation Movement of Liberia for Democracy
UN	United Nations
UNOMIL	United Nations Observer Mission in Liberia

Foreword

Armed international interventions, justified on humanitarian grounds, have been among the most controversial episodes of world affairs since the end of the Cold War. Why should such interventions be controversial? Are not international humanitarian actions justifiable *prima facie*? It is because humanitarian grounds for such military actions are not explicitly sanctioned by the United Nations Charter, which privileges the doctrine of non-intervention, the inherent right of self defense, and the Security Council's responsibility to preserve international peace and security. Various Security Council Resolutions that justify armed international intervention make reference to human rights, but only in the context of efforts to uphold international peace and security. Sovereign states and international organizations have done the same in exercising their right of self-defense. But none of that calls into question, much less does it undermine or change, the fundamental principle of state sovereignty, which has been and continues to be the cornerstone of international law. The constitutive fact that state sovereignty is "the essential pillar upon which the architecture of international society is built" explains why "humanitarian intervention is the most controversial subject in international affairs" if it seeks or has the effect of undermining that arrangement. Any contemplated departure and movement away from that fundamental principle is fraught with traps, snares and delusions, as many recent humanitarian interventions in various parts of the world bear witness to.

Mourtada Déme is undoubtedly correct in interpreting UN norms and practice as, on balance, "realistic and prudent" rather than idealistic and progressive. The fathers of the United Nations who met in San Francisco in 1945, immediately following the most calamitous war in human history which involved unprecedented humanitarian disasters, were determined to endorse the fundamental principles of equal state sovereignty, territorial integrity and non-intervention as the foundation of the new world organization. That was because they were responding to the many acts of armed intervention by Fascist Italy in Ethiopia, by Nazi Germany across Europe, and by Imperialist Japan in Asia and the Pacific which precipitated that war and provoked the allied war effort. All those interventions involved massive human rights violations and some of them acts of forced labor and genocidal murder on an unimaginable scale.

Armed international intervention, as traditionally understood, is an instrument of foreign policy calculated to serve the interests of states or alliances, and it should not be surprising if those same interests are in play in acts of humanitarian intervention, because "states are not intrinsically altruistic" and cannot be such—even when they strive to defend human rights and pursue humanitarian causes. Perhaps there is a place for altruism in world affairs, but it could not be the only place or even a large place, and all of the time it will be subject, sooner or later, to other considerations, the most important of which is self-interest.

That was certainly the case in Liberia in the 1990s, as the author makes abundantly clear. Here was a state that had been destroyed and its population subjected to a Hobbesian war "of all against all" by avaricious, merciless, utterly brutal and unforgiving armed gangs and their warlords. When an international rescue operation to save the Liberian people was finally mounted by neighboring West African states, it turned out that the intervening forces exploited the situation rather than saving the people, and contributed to further human rights violations, by making arms available, out of regard for their own interests, to "ill-disciplined militias" and "unaccountable mercenaries" who used the weapons "to attack and massacre civilians." In Liberia the interveners became part of the problem rather than the solution. How that happened is explained in Déme's groundbreaking study.

If there is an international solution to the problem of massive human rights violations in sovereign states, Déme argues that it is not to be found in efforts of so-called humanitarian intervention, which all-too-often are overwhelmed by the many practical difficulties and obstacles involved in trying to save people by means of international armed force. That happens even in situations where armed interventionists have the best of intentions and the greatest discipline. In the 1999 humanitarian intervention in Kosovo, NATO air forces succeeded in halting ethnic cleansing of the Moslem population carried out by Serbian armed forces and local Serbian militias on the orders of Yugoslav President Slobodan Milosevich. But in the course of that more or less successful humanitarian intervention, NATO bombs killed many innocent civilians. Even when intentions are relatively pure, the consequences are always something else, especially if armed force is employed, with all its uncertainties and dangers for the people involved, both soldiers and civilians. Armed force is at the heart of humanitarian intervention. And morally speaking, the anticipated consequences of military action are something that can never be ignored or dismissed, not even when the war aim is noble and humane.

The starting place of most humanitarian disasters since the end of the Cold War has been the failure of states, or their perversion by malevolent rulers and ruthless regimes. That is the obverse side of the fact that human rights can only be protected with assurance in effectively organized, democratic states which respect the rule of law and the sanctity and dignity of people. If there is an international solution to problems of massive human rights violations in abusive or failed states it can only be sought in a renewed appreciation that human rights protections require viable states to do the protecting, and international actions to promote state viability. Rather than undermining sovereign states or arguing that state sovereignty must be interfered with in order to protect human rights, in fact what is required is the promotion of state sovereignty and good governance based on the principle of international reciprocity. The international society of sovereign states must be strengthened, not weakened. That important message from Mourtada Déme is both timely and necessary to correct the widespread misunderstanding, which proved seriously harmful in Kosovo and calamitous in Liberia, that human rights can be safeguarded by international military action without the dangers and chaos and suffering that armed intervention almost inevitably brings about.

Robert Jackson
Professor of International Relations and Political Science
Boston University

Preface

The conflict between international norms and real world suffering became a crisis point in Liberia in the 1990s. During the 1989–1997 war, the Economic Community of West African States (ECOWAS) and the United Nations (UN) used the Liberian crisis to revise the legally established principle of non-intervention in order to authorize outside interference in a sovereign country. They portrayed it as a significant departure from past practices to a new model of partnership for the resolution of future crises. This book analyzes these justifications and developments. I argue that the intervention was extremely controversial because legal precepts set out in ECOWAS instruments, the UN Charter, and the International Court of Justice's interpretation of these principles do not, in fact, authorize intervention on humanitarian grounds. Despite the sophisticated arguments and efforts of international lawyers to reformulate international law and to persuade others that their own morality should become the shared morality embodied in international instruments, humanitarian intervention is still *jus incognitum*. On moral grounds, not only did the justifications advanced appear to be half-truth, but the ways of expressing condemnation for human rights violations do not include the use of force against a sovereign state. Finally, the intervention was politically unsuccessful and its developments uncertain. The Liberian conflict demonstrates rather the wisdom of the older concept of limited intervention because the problem of the West African crisis was not so much that the principles of international law and politics were outdated, but that they were not respected. One of the most important needs for both the UN and regional organizations in maintenance of peace is to work within the legal framework of the Charter.

Of equal importance, justifications for the need to protect regional security are weak. Although some legal basis exists under ECOWAS instruments and general principles of international law, the argument for regional security is undermined by the role played by member states that assisted, supported and financed the armed groups and militias. Thus, non-intervention remains preferable to the façade of mutual assistance. The regional approach proposed by ECOWAS and the UN is a gross oversimplification, and falsely presumes that regional approaches to failed states in Africa are superior to wider multilateral efforts. While regional organizations present some advantages, their suitability for assuming primary responsibility for security is questionable. The financial and logistical difficulties experienced in African conflicts, the fragility of government dependence on outside forces including mercenaries, the divisions, conflicting interests among member states of ECOWAS and the subsequent partisan involvement of the states exposed the limitations of the sub-regional approach for effective action. ECOWAS is not yet a coherent organization, and lacks effectiveness. There is a critical gap between the adoption of normative instruments at the regional level and their implementation. Regional integration cannot be shaped by grandiose meetings, communiqués, divided individual leaders, and a foreign policy of lip service.

Finally, the general argument of the book can be read as an invitation to address the questions at the level they should be addressed : domestic politics. The core problem is not a redefinition of sovereignty or its obsolescence, but the failure of African states to penetrate the real lives of their citizens and protect their fundamental human rights. Who can claim that the interventions undertaken in Liberia and elsewhere in Africa have been successful in protecting human rights? The attempts to protect human rights by arms have proved to be a disaster. In West Africa, external powers colluded with oppressive regimes and profited from arms sales and diamond purchases. Armed activities have failed protecting civilians from harm inflicted by militias, government troops and even "peace-keepers" accused of many violations of human rights that include sexual exploitation of children.

Should human rights remain only a subject of discussion or do they need to be implemented in order to improve the way in which victims are treated? Frankly, no enlightened person will disagree that all people are entitled to enjoy human rights irrespective of characteristics such as race, religion, sex, nationality, social class or political belief. International and nongovernmental organizations have played an important role in raising consciousness through the adoption of remarkable documents. But the effectiveness and the credibility of human rights go beyond ratifications. They depend on the domestic legal and political systems that comply with and implement them. The global message contained in international instruments and the achievements of regional goals depend on the *volonté* of the state.

This book has its origins in my Ph.D. dissertation completed at Boston University. In the course of writing it, I have incurred many debts. I am grateful to the intellectual stimulation and sustained support of Edouard Bustin and Cathal Nolan. Robert Jackson has, as usual, been a starting-place for ideas and his work has had a strong influence on me. I am also grateful to Benjamin Holtzman, Dissertations Editor at Routledge, for expressing an intention to publish my work. His professionalism had a very encouraging effect. I also want to express my gratitude to Sarah Blackmon, Eleanor Chan, and Carey Nershi for their valuable assistance. Some friends made useful suggestions and I should particularly like to acknowledge Kofi Asimpi and Masse Ndiaye, who read and commented upon various texts of the manuscript. Needless to say, none of the above shares my responsibility for any errors of fact or interpretation. The African Studies Center and the West African Research Association provided funding to support my work and a welcoming environment. I am also grateful to the staff of the African Studies Library at Boston University and to the Director, Gretchen Walsh for her assistance. Racha Aribarg, John Gay, Tom Johnson, Brendan McDermott, Jurga Poskevisiute, Wendy Rodwin, read early drafts and provided insightful comments.

I have other friends to thank: Ibra Baro, Alioune Diop, Issagha Fofana, Olivier Mercoli, Fatima Ndoye, Reginald Pryor, and Ousmane Seck. I am indebted to Dr. H. A. Crosby Forbes, my mentor for wonderful times together and stimulating conversation on history and philosophy. Colette Dornelly's love, humor and support were essential to me. Finally my greatest debt is to my family. My sister Aissata, and my brother Bachir, were constant and inexhaustible sources of comfort. Through the years, Mimi Kane has become a confidante. Mansour E. Kane has always urged me to persevere. My parents gave me the opportunities that made possible my career and to advance this far in life. They have my deepest thanks.

M.D.
Boston

Introduction

Humanitarian intervention is the most controversial subject in international affairs. The topic is at the center of a conflict of norms between international human rights law on the one hand, and the principles of state sovereignty, domestic jurisdiction, and non-intervention, on the other. The same complexity arises when it comes to examining the ethical arguments: authorizing humanitarian intervention will open the floodgates to anarchy and chaos, while at the same time it is morally difficult to restrain from intervening in cases of genocide or widespread torture, especially when the absence of state control is the primary cause of disastrous human and material consequences. Today international responses to internal conflicts remain confusing and uncertain, in large part because of the absence of a clearly defined doctrine.

This book analyzes the justifications of humanitarian intervention and its effects within a country with failed government, by focusing on the Liberian case. The Liberian crisis is relevant to this study for many reasons. First, it represents a perfect example in terms of the broader theoretical debate. Second, the conflict exhibited all the problems of intervention, as well as the manifestations of post-Cold War intra-state conflict: breakdown of governance, state collapse, political fragmentation, rise of vigilantes, proliferation of small arms, an uncertain response from the United Nations, a quasi-indifference of the international community, and the involvement of a regional body to address the security threat. As a result, Liberia provides a useful empirical basis for analyzing the complexities of the intervention and its subsequent developments.

In 1990 rebels descended on Monrovia, the Liberian capital, to depose the government of Master Sargeant Samuel Doe. The National Patriotic Front, led by Charles Taylor, emerged triumphant after a brutal war that displaced hundreds of thousands of people from their homes and destroyed all civil institutions, which created a complete breakdown of law and order, and brought about a humanitarian crisis with atrocities and massive violation of human rights. The refugee crisis and the proliferation of armed groups in Sierra Leone and Guinea threatened to destabilize other countries in the sub-region. On August 24, 1990, after much delay due to internal divisions, the leaders of the Economic Community of West African States (ECOWAS) sent troops into Liberia and justified their decision to intervene on humanitarian grounds, the need to protect regional peace and security, and the restoration of order in a country in chaos. Although the interest of the United Nations in Liberia in the early stages was mainly carried through the UN General Assembly, the organization was determined to support the initiatives of ECOWAS and portrayed it as an example that should be followed by other regional organizations. In fact, the war in Liberia was one of the first civil conflicts where the United Nations, ECOWAS, and to some extent, the African Union (formerly the Organization of African Unity), revised the legal principle of non-intervention to authorize external interference in a sovereign country.

The justifications on the basis of humanitarian intervention and regional insecurity should be treated separately. Although the pertinent legal dispositions contained in the United Nations Charter and ECOWAS instruments on regional security will be discussed, the notion is relatively clear. Regional security is a form of collective defense based on pacts and alliances of mutual defense against outside attacks guaranteeing that an aggression against any member state of the region will be resisted by all the other states whose contribution to the common defense may be required. The same cannot be said about humanitarian intervention, which is a much more complicated idea that needs to be defined before going further.

DEFINITION AND CONTROVERSIES

The ECOWAS justifications based on humanitarian intervention are all the more uncertain and divisive as the very permissibility of such action is a theme of great dispute in international law and politics: how can territorial sovereignty, regarded legally as the cornerstone of international relations, non-interference in the domestic affairs of foreign states, and the prohibition of the use of armed force, all stipulated in the United Nations Charter, be reconciled with the effective protection of human rights?

DEFINING HUMANITARIAN INTERVENTION

Intervention is a *portmanteau* term, a "puzzle,"[1] an ambiguous concept of international politics,[2] an "unscientific concept."[3] The topic covers a variety of situations (diffuse, direct, and indirect) and actions (economic coercion such as sanctions, boycotts, embargoes or political conditionalties). To complicate matters further, intervention is "a built-in" in international politics. Hedley Bull, in one of his last comments on the subject, had the intuition that, "with the growing legal and moral recognition of human rights," the problem of humanitarian intervention will remain with us for a long time. In 1984, he wrote: "Ultimately, we have a rule of non-intervention because unilateral intervention threatens the harmony and concord of the society of sovereign states. . . . If, however, an intervention itself expresses the collective will of the society of states, it may be carried out without bringing that harmony and concord into jeopardy."[4]

Since Bull's death in May, 1985, we have noted a revival of disputes on the subject of humanitarian intervention among philosophers, legal scholars, and political scientists. Robert O. Keohane stated, " . . . it is a little bit like crying fire in a crowded theater: it can create a clear and present danger to everyone within earshot."[5] It is therefore necessary to limit the subject.

In traditional international law, intervention is seen in normative terms. It is first and foremost a breach of the sovereignty of the target state;[6] a violation of its independence and its sovereignty. In the view of most traditionalist international law scholars, intervention is a dictatorial interference in the domestic jurisdiction of a sovereign state. According to one comprehensive definition, intervention is an "activity undertaken by a state . . . a group of states or an international organization which interferes coercively in the domestic affairs of another state."[7] In line with this definition, intervention occurs when an external party violates the territorial integrity of a state by using physical force in one form or another. Intervention will be understood as a forcible interference in the affairs of another state.

Intervention is said to be humanitarian under two conditions: a coercive intrusion in the domestic affairs of another country with the objective of stopping massive violations of human rights.[8] According to Murphy, "Humanitarian intervention is the threat or use of force by a state, group of states, or international organization primarily for the purpose of protecting the nationals of the target state from widespread deprivations of internationally recognized human rights."[9] Holzgrefe's definition on the subject is very similar. Humanitarian intervention is "the threat or use of force across state borders by a state (or group of states) aimed at preventing or ending widespread and grave violations of the fundamental human rights of individuals other than its own citizens, without the permission of the state within whose territory force is applied."[10] To what extent do legal norms support humanitarian intervention?

THE ARGUMENTS FOR HUMANITARIAN INTERVENTION

There is not yet an incontrovertible norm of international law that authorizes humanitarian intervention. Indeed, under international law, the use of force for the resolution of controversies is prohibited. Supporters of the so-called right of humanitarian intervention justify their position by interpreting international law, mostly the dispositions on human rights in the United Nations Charter. One major problem with that justification is that the UN Charter is a mix of realism and idealism. Therefore, when it comes to interpretation, realists and idealists, interventionists and non-interventionists can find in the same legal documents arguments to support their case, because the debate is often manipulated by scholars with different philosophical and moral biases.

Nevertheless, the proponents of the *droit d'ingérence* argue that when a state outrages the conscience of mankind by its behavior, it loses the privileges offered by the principle of non-intervention.[11] Although the United Nations prohibits the use of force, the principle agrees to some exceptions.[12] Another proponent of humanitarian intervention had argued that "gross violations of human rights are considered to be matters of international rather than domestic concern, and to represent possible threats to the peace."[13] But, except that case, advocates of humanitarian intervention justify their position either by reinterpreting state sovereignty or by pointing out the multiplication of instruments protecting human rights.[14] In reinterpreting the concept of sovereignty, supporters of the right to intervene argue that state sovereignty is meaningless when applied to dictatorships or undemocratic leaders and should be vested in the individuals.[15] According to Nicholas Onuf, sovereignty is anachronistic.[16] Military intervention for the promotion of human rights constitutes a radical and revolutionary revision of state sovereignty. It is maintained that the right to go to war to defend the oppressed exists,[17] because state sovereignty, in the words of Fernando Tesòn, is 'statist rhetoric,' 'Hegelian Myth.'[18]

In the same vein, other analysts believe that because the state is a servant of its people, the way in which individuals are treated within their country should be a subject of legitimate concern for other governments.[19] Therefore, international law should be constructed on a new foundation and take ethical imperatives into consideration.[20] International law, it is submitted, should adopt an approach of solidarity, fitting not only the interests of states, but also the aspirations of human beings. Consequently, states have the duty to promote justice beyond their borders, and when capable, "they are the guardianship of human rights everywhere" and should be given the right to stop massive violations of human rights. As Nicolas J. Wheeler argues, "States that massively violate human rights should forfeit their right to be treated as legitimate sovereigns, thereby morally entitling other states to use force to stop the oppression."[21] It necessitates, as Richard Falk advocates, "dethroning the statist paradigm" where people are defined in relation to their state rather than in relation to each other and the wider global community.[22] This kind of international responsibility, to be sure, does not exist anywhere in international relations but was echoed by Michael Reisman, who wrote:

> One can no longer simply condemn externally motivated actions, aimed at removing an unpopular government and permitting the con- sultation or implementation of the popular will, as per se violations of sovereignty, without inquiring whether and under what conditions, that will was being suppressed, and how the external action will affect the expression and implementation of popular sovereignty.[23]

Similarly, David J. Scheffer has put forward the view that morality is a legal basis for humanitarian intervention: "To argue today that norms of sover- eignty, non-use of force, and the sanctity of internal affairs are paramount to the collective human rights of people, whose life and well-being are at risk, is to avoid the hard questions of international law and to ignore the march of history."[24] But to ignore "the march of history" is not a substan- tial criticism because no one knows what the future holds. On the contrary, history is neither decipherable nor determined. History is yet to be written. Ultimately, the common strand of these opinions is to challenge state sover- eignty, and thus allow intervention when a government of a territory is committing extensive violations of the rights of its citizens. But even on moral grounds *stricto sensu* these arguments are refutable: the pursuit of pre-established known and accepted laws is the foundation of all legalistic morality.[25] In a diverse world, where a court for morals is unthinkable, the moral precept is to give effect to the law and in doing so, the international society, as argued here, is pursuing the moral choice of certainty rather than uncertainty.

A major problem with the reformulation of international law as basis for humanitarian intervention is that most of the "new readings" on the sub- ject is manipulative doctrine. The writings of publicists are among the sources of international law, but they are subsidiary means for the determination of such law. There is no doubt that individual writers such as Hugo Grotius, "the miracle of Holland," or the great Vattel, among others, have earned international reputation and have had a significant impact in the development of such law. But, for the controversial subject of humanitarian intervention, subjectivity enters into consideration in the formulation of juristic opinion. Indeed some publicists, lawyers and scholars, proponents of humanitarian intervention, see themselves to be propagating not only new, but better views. Thus, they often fail to provide a passive appraisal of the law. Their reformulations, if anything, are secondary in the determination of applicable law. They are in fundamental contradiction with the general rule of interpretation of international law that requires that dispositions be interpreted in authenticity. Article 31 of the Vienna Convention requires "a treaty be interpreted in good faith and in accordance with the ordinary meaning to be given to the terms of the treaty in their context and in light of its object and purpose." Article 2 of the UN Charter is clear: its approach is non-interventionist.

In addition to reinterpreting international law and sovereignty, proponents of humanitarian intervention argue that the conventions and legal instruments that have, under the United Nations auspices, directed international attention to the fate of individuals in international affairs are a legal basis for intervention. They appeared on the global scene, for the first time, with the Universal Declaration of Human Rights in 1948. Enthusiasm and optimism led to the ratification of a plethora of accords such as the Convention on the Prevention and Punishment of the Crime of Genocide (1948), the Geneva Conventions on the Protection of Victims of War (1949), the Convention on the Elimination of all Forms of Racial Discrimination (1965), the International Covenant on Civil and Political Rights (1966), the International Covenant on Economic, Social and Cultural Rights (1966), the Convention against Torture and Other Cruel, Inhuman Degrading Treatment or Punishment (1979), among others. Advocates of humanitarian intervention claimed that the protection of human rights was one of the *raison d'être* of the United Nations and these instruments represent a luminous and moving expression of human dignity.[26]

In fact, notwithstanding the elegance of the argument, these conventions were intended to develop a normative paradigm that reduces the traditional *domaine réservé*. Despite the imperfections of law, it was expected that these multilateral agreements would strengthen the legitimacy of human rights at the international level. By signing these agreements, states accept legal responsibility under the Charter, and under general principles of international law, to execute their obligations toward their citizens and other signatories in good faith. For the General Assembly, these conventions, especially those concluded under the UN auspices, give expression to the moral conscience of humankind and represent "rules concerning the basic rights of the human person."[27] In other words, sovereignty can be limited and the state is required to promote human rights. Some of these rights deserve the highest protection. Such rights include the dispositions of law relating to torture and unlawful killing; the law of armed conflict on the protection of civilians, or the 1948 Genocide Convention, which specifies that any contracting state "may call upon the competent organs of the United Nations to take such action under the Charter of the United Nations as they consider appropriate for the prevention and suppression of acts of genocide . . ."[28]

The International Court of Justice in 1970 reaffirmed that the obligations of states toward the international community as a whole include the protection of the individual against the crime of genocide as well as the protection of the principles and rules concerning basic human rights. Among these international instruments, the Convention on the Prevention and Punishment of the Crime of Genocide is the only one which provides in the text provisions that can be interpreted as a legal basis for intervention when it stipulates that the parties may "call upon the competent organs of the United Nations to take . . . action . . . they consider appropriate for the prevention and suppression of acts of genocide." In the words of the International Court of Justice, the protection of these basic rights is the concern of all states: "In view of the importance of the rights involved, all states can be held to have a legal interest in their protection; they are obligations *erga omnes* . . ."[29] But, even in this case, the original intent was that the individual bears responsibility under the convention of genocide. The targets were individuals. Following the holocaust, the objective was to bring the perpetrators of the worst moral crimes to justice. Here it is noteworthy that the perpetrator is not necessarily a state's government or its military, but may be a guerilla organization, rebel or terrorist groups, or an international organization such as a UN peacekeeping force.

Genocide, regardless of the authority under which it is committed, is ultimately planned and conducted by humans. The intention to persecute all *génocidaire* is made explicit in Article 4 which stipulates: "Persons committing genocide or any of the other acts enumerated in article III shall be punished, whether they are constitutionally responsible rulers, public officials or private individuals." The text was purposefully intended to apply to all individuals. In other words, national responsibility, as exercised by a head of state or government, or a member of parliament does not constitute legal protection of any sort to escape prosecution. One can also note that even in the case of genocide, engaging state responsibility under the convention has politically proven to be very difficult. Member states of the UN hesitate to indicate other member states, or to intervene: it is what one saw in Rwanda. Human rights defense organizations have voiced these criticisms and estimated that the definition under Article 2 of the Convention is too restrictive, that the intention *génocidaire* is very difficult to prove and that grave acts would not fall under such a definition.[30] As for other instruments on human rights, their legal status will be discussed further, but suffice it to say that it is also hard for an international court to convict a government of human rights violations. While advocates and activists of "global society" can condemn openly, these criticisms are not a legal basis for humanitarian intervention.

In most conventions, comfort was found in the acknowledgment by governments of their legal obligations. It was an optimistic view. When massive violations of human rights occur, retaliatory measures and reprisals can be taken in political and diplomatic ways. States can retain their bilateral aid and they can apply embargos. The truth is that sovereignty repudiates the existence of a worldwide international police force whose role is to enforce human rights. Nevertheless, because the UN Charter can support an idealist as well as a realist interpretation, Secretary General Kofi Annan endorsed the view that the international community should not stand by when governments mistreat their citizens. He asserts, "the Charter was never meant as a license for governments to trample on human rights and human dignity. Sovereignty implies responsibility, not just power."[31] The Independent Commission on International Issues, the London-based bureau on public awareness of humanitarian affairs, reached a similar conclusion: "Sovereignty need not conflict with humanitarian concerns if States can be brought to define their interests beyond the short term . . . The interests of common humanity which transcend national boundaries are not a menace to the vital interests of States."[32] But the extent to which a state loses the protection afforded by the principle of non-intervention when it fails to promote human rights is difficult to find in international law. Despite the 'generous' intentions of its champions, the concept of humanitarian intervention raises many doubts because altruism is not the essence of international politics. The Secretary General had on several occasions witnessed the lack of international commitment to altruistic actions, Liberia being a case in point.

ARGUMENTS AGAINST HUMANITARIAN INTERVENTION

Authors who oppose the principle of intervention recognize to states an absolute right and a protection against any form of foreign interference. They have clear legal dispositions as well as authoritative statements on their side. Humanitarian intervention is a violation of international law. What transpires inside the borders of a sovereign state is no one else's affair.

The principle of non-intervention is the cornerstone of the United Nations Charter, which strongly prohibits intervention in article 2(4): "All Members shall refrain in their international relations from the threat or use of force against the territorial integrity and political independence of any state, or in any manner inconsistent with the purposes of the United Nations." According to Michael Akehurst, " . . . the promotion of human rights is one of the purposes of the United Nations . . ." but he also argues, "[the] Charter intended to prohibit the use of force except in the case of self-defense or under the direction of the Security Council acting under Chapter VII of the Charter."[33]

Considering the varied backgrounds of the member states and their different understanding of human rights, the UN Charter adopted a realistic and prudent approach. Latin American countries, which witnessed different types of foreign interventions, defended a non-interventionist approach at the United Nations. Indeed, the legal framework for their position was already crafted well before the advent of the UN by Argentinan jurists Carlos Calvo Louis Maria Drago, and later by Genaro Estrada.[34] The General Assembly's interpretation of the principle of non-intervention was close to the Latin American experience, i.e., near absolute. In multiple declarations, the UN General Assembly forbids all states to intervene directly or indirectly in the internal or external affairs of other states. Or, by virtue of the principle of equal sovereignty, each state is permitted to decide freely the choice of its political, economic, social and cultural system.[35]

Interpreting the dispositions on the non-use of force in international relations, the International Court of Justice estimated that humanitarian intervention does not constitute a valid limitation to the prohibition, and strongly reinforced the positions adopted by the General Assembly, as upheld in the following view:

> Adherence by a State to any particular doctrine does not constitute a violation of customary international law; to hold otherwise would make nonsense of the fundamental principle of State sovereignty, on which the whole international law rests, and the freedom of choice of the political, social, economic and cultural system of a State. Consequently, Nicaragua's domestic policy options, even assuming that they correspond to the description given of them by the Congress finding, cannot justify on the legal plane the various actions the Respondent complained of.[36]

Politically, developing states, and at least two members of the UN Security Council, generally tend to view human rights issues as an internal matter and intervention as a violation of international law. In the context of the North-South debate on human rights, it has been argued, and supported by African states, that human rights have to be understood in a social context but are not universal (the Universal Declaration of Human rights was not adopted unanimously). The vigorous debate over the universality of human rights still continues and is based either on the argument of cultural diversity or on philosophical skepticism regarding the idea of human rights itself.[37] Countries that adopt a non-interventionist view are suspicious about the label 'humanitarian.' After all, the doctrine that inspired European colonialism has been justified by *les Lois d'humanité*.[38]

Intervention is often an instrument of foreign policy that seeks to achieve specific goals determined by decision-makers.[39] The realist tradition of Hans Morgenthau teaches that interactions between states are anarchic and universal moral principles cannot be applied to the actions of the state.[40] Hence, the primary obligation of statesmen is to promote the interests of the national society it represents, the well being of its peoples.[41] Egoism best describes the morality of states that always act in pursuit of their interests. The truth is that in many conflicts, there is a reluctance to intervene in the absence of vital national benefits. When the interest of Western countries is not self-evident, the humanitarian impulse has low priority. In 1999 the World Food Program announced that it would have to curtail its programs for two millions refugees in Sierra Leone, Liberia, and Guinea having received less than 20 percent of requested funding. At the same time Randolph Kent, who moved from UN programs in the Balkans to East Africa noted that the United Nations High Commissioner for Refugees (UNHCR) expenditures per refugee in the Balkans was eleven times as high as in Africa. "The hundreds of millions of dollars spent on Kosovo refugees and the crush of aid agencies eager to spend it was almost an obscenity."[42]

If states' actions are egoistic, how do interventionists know when intervention is humanitarian? If the outcome is humanitarian, does it matter whether the intent is altruistic or self-serving? Can intervention by a powerful state ever be viewed as philanthropic? Most interventions are driven by other motives. Humanitarian intervention is based on power rather than on legal right or international solidarity, and it can therefore serve as an exercise of might in which the strong uses moral argument as a cover for state interest.[43] Robert Tucker has a long time ago argued that "the nature of international society . . . makes a disparity between principle and practice inevitable." Therefore, the label humanitarian intervention is often a form of political dominance of the weak by the strong,[44] and authors have been searching for true examples of humanitarian intervention.[45] In the case of Liberia, it is ironic for Nigeria (a military dictatorship in 1990) to task ECOMOG with "creating the necessary conditions for free and fair elections." If for the past half-century interventions based on human solidarity are so limited; it is state power or interest that is behind most interventions. Because states are not intrinsically altruistic, intervention is legally and morally contradictory, and this lends more weight to the argument of state sovereignty as the essential pillar upon which the architecture of international society is built.[46] In most cases, morality has played an instrumental political role, as illustrated in the justifications advanced for intervening in Liberia.

THE CONTEXT OF THE LIBERIAN INTERVENTION

Scholars have provided a comprehensive examination of the historical roots of the Liberian conflict.[47] The American Colonization Society resettled freed slaves on Liberia's shores in the 1820s. These "Americo-Liberians,"[48] who constituted only about five per cent of the population, dominated the political, economic and social life of the country for over 150 years. In a bloody military coup in 1980, Master-Sergeant Samuel Doe killed President Tolbert, his associates, and the country's top politicians. This event marked the end of the Americo-Liberian rule. The majority of the population initially welcomed the coup.

Throughout the 1980s, like many African regimes, Doe relied on the support of a major power for foreign aid, in this case, the United States. As there was international pressure on African regimes to promote political participation, elections were presented as a precondition for transition to democracy. Doe became president in 1985, following contested elections. As expected, the 1985 election did not by itself constitute a guarantee to democracy or to good governance. Human rights violations continued to be part of the daily life of Liberians.[49] These violations, together with political discrimination and economic exclusion, further precipitated the conflict.

In December 1989, Charles Taylor, who had escaped from jail in Massachusetts, invaded the country from Ivory Coast with his 200 followers of the National Patriotic Front of Liberia (NPFL) with the objective of overthrowing the Doe government.[50] All sides in the conflict were accused of attacks, murder and torture of innocent civilians.[51] On July 2, Taylor launched his attack against Monrovia and displayed significant savagery. By August 1990, Doe's government had lost control of Liberia territory and his regime was confined to government buildings. He rejected the widespread demands that he resign. In September 1990, he was assassinated by Prince Johnson, a leader of the Independent National Patriotic Front of Liberia (INFPL) rebel group, which had come into existence after a split from Taylor's NPFL. After Doe's death, the INPFL directed the fight against their former NPFL partners. Combatants from all three groups looted Liberia's economic infrastructure. Civil authority ceased to exist, and some ECOWAS states feared that the war would increase refugee flow and worsen political instability in their already bankrupted and ruined states.

As the fighting escalated and the international community expressed marginal concern, a group of five ECOWAS members established at the insistence of Nigeria's President Ibrahim Babangida the Standing Mediation Committee (SMC) in April 1990 to resolve the conflict. For about two more months the war was still raging and the ECOWAS Monitoring Group (ECOMOG) was created on August 7 of the same year. It immediately faced the problem of political disunity, as some countries, such as Burkina Faso and Togo, openly condemned the intervention as an intrusion in the internal affairs of a sovereign country, while other member states such as Sénégal, remained neutral. More importantly, there was a clash between the interests of Nigeria and those of other West African States, notably Côte d'Ivoire.[52] ECOMOG also faced other political divisions since most of the contributors were Anglophone states: Nigeria, Ghana, Sierra Leone, and the Gambia. Guinea at the outset was the only Francophone state which participated. It has also been reported that other African countries, such as Zaïre and Ethiopia, who were members of the Security Council at the time, were not enthusiastic about bringing up the matter before the Security Council. It has been argued that most African countries wished to avoid creating a precedent, and therefore prevented the Liberian issue from being scheduled before the Security Council.[53]

Despite political disunity and these divisions, the Standing Mediation Committee comprising five of the fifteen states,[54] gave ECOMOG a mandate to conduct military operations for the purpose of restoring peace and stability in Liberia:

> The failure of the warring parties to cease hostilities has led to the massive destruction of property and the massacre by all parties of thousands of civilians, including foreign nationals, women and children . . . contrary to all standards of civilized behavior . . . Presently there is a government in Liberia, which cannot govern, and contending factions, which are holding the entire population as hostage, depriving them of food, health facilities and other basic necessities of life. These developments have traumatized the Liberian population and greatly shocked

the people of the sub-region and the rest of the international community. They have also led to hundreds of thousands of Liberians being displaced and made refugees in neighboring countries, and the spilling of hostilities into neighboring countries.[55]

ECOMOG was deployed on August 23, 1990 to end the conflict.

What role did the international community play during this period? In fact, there was no international response to the war either from the Western countries or from the OAU. No major power expressed a desire to intervene militarily. The OAU has always opposed military interference in the internal affairs of a fellow African state without request, but for the first time its Secretary General, Salim Ahmed Salim, welcomed the intervention.[56] The UN paid little attention to the suffering of Liberians. Not until January 1991, thirteen months after it started, did the Security Council publicly comment on the war.[57] The international organization passed its first resolution only in November 1992, determining that the situation in Liberia was a threat to international peace, especially in West Africa, and called on the parties to respect the Yamoussoukro accords.[58] These accords were the result of a series of meetings held in Yamoussoukro, Côte d'Ivoire, between June and October 1991. Between 1992 and 1997, the UN passed several other resolutions, all supportive of the ECOWAS initiatives, but the international organization played a secondary role.

This form of partnership was unprecedented, and when the conflict was officially "over" in 1997, the UN and ECOWAS officials estimated that they had established a new approach for future cooperation that could enhance the role of regional organizations in their future peace operations. Two major developments resulted from that approach. The first was the adoption by ECOWAS of a security mechanism at its summit in Lomé, Togo, in December 1999, to institutionalize the experience of ECOMOG in Liberia. The second was the decision by the UN to generate a West Africa office in Dakar and to appoint a special representative of the Secretary General for solidifying the regional approach. The new strategy is aimed at developing the capabilities of ECOWAS to play a central role in humanitarian initiatives thereby creating a "new framework" of intra conflict resolution in Africa and reinforcing the well known slogan "African solutions to African problems."

The argument presented here is that the Liberian case provides a perfect example for understanding the intricacies of intervention in a 'domestic' conflict, especially in West Africa. Critically examined, however, the Liberian conflict does not supersede the current political arrangement and the legal doctrine of non-intervention. While the Liberian War set a precedent on the issue of cooperation between the UN and regional organizations, it did not provide convincing answers to the perennial difficulties that have been the hallmark of these conflicts. Simply put, there exists a myriad of hurdles involved in fostering an African regional initiative because of the absence of viable states capable of carrying the global message on human rights and the regional objectives.

The approach attempting to challenge the traditional legal structure by calling into question the concept of sovereignty in order to permit the protection of human rights is flawed. In a sense, the debate about humanitarian intervention and state sovereignty is badly expressed, because it posits an excessive opposition between human rights and the state. State sovereignty and human rights do not necessarily stand in opposition to one another. The state is the most important protector of human rights, probably the only effective protector, if one is talking about substance. Recent internal conflicts have proven that human rights are more in danger in the absence of a state. Therefore, in the West African context, the question should not be to undermine the state as the legitimate source of governance and authority, but to strengthen it, to make it work, because authority properly understood refers to the rule of law.

Advocates of humanitarian intervention have focused their criticisms on state sovereignty and have argued that leaders who grossly assault human rights should not be allowed to shield themselves behind the principle of sovereignty.[59] But sovereignty need not be antithetical to human rights, and the idea that sovereignty is incompatible with effective protection of human rights is misleading. On the contrary, it is the antithesis of tyranny, and sovereignty properly understood, protects human rights. There is a fundamental difference between sovereignty as the supreme authority, which is necessary for a political community to exist, and the absolutist use and abuse of state sovereignty. In fact, what is "final and absolute" is not sovereignty itself, but authority.[60] Sovereignty can be voluntarily limited by a variety of international agreements, which often include human rights. Authority is not dictatorship, as practiced by many regimes, but refers to the state's legal or constitutional independence vis-à-vis other states.[61] In this sense, sovereignty is "final and absolute authority in a political community."[62] Otherwise put, it refers to "the single governing authority which is acknowledged to be supreme over all other authorities within a certain territorial jurisdiction and is independent of all foreign authorities."[63] These definitions have three implications: first, because a sovereign state is independent it makes its own laws and no other entity can nullify these; second, the state is not subject to an external competing authority; third, intervention in the internal affairs of a sovereign state is not permitted. But supreme authority does not mean that a government can claim that it is lawful to exterminate or slaughter its own population on the grounds that it is sovereign.

In the domain of human rights, especially those adopted by the UN Charter, the scope of sovereignty is also defined by obligations in which states have freely entered, so they must respect them in a likewise sovereign manner. Otherwise, they violate the oldest principle of international law, *Pacta Sunt Servanda*. The plethora of international legal instruments has modified the *domaine réservé* but this does not necessarily mean a diminution of state sovereignty. Nor does it indicate a fundamental contradiction between the very nature of state sovereignty and the existence of these agreements. When a state cooperates internationally and implements the fundamental norms of human rights that it has freely endorsed, its *jus regendi* is neither affected nor weakened by the multiplication of treaties, because it can release itself from treaty obligations either by virtue of provisions for termination or under the principle *rebus sic stantibus.*[64]

If implementation and enforcement are the very essence of human rights, then the state is vital. Despite the increase of human rights instruments at the international level, there are no enforcement or implementation measures attached to these declarations, and most of the time, states take the appropriate legislative and other national measures necessary to achieve the stated objectives. Thus, states do matter. States are not the only actors of international politics, but they are paramount, despite the multiplication of Non-Governmental Organizations (NGOs), and the debate among scholars about their importance, especially in the context of globalization.[65] Non-state actors have played an important role in bringing the subject of human rights to the global agenda. However they cannot substitute for the state; at the best they can influence state behavior.

The state is *summum bonum,* the greatest good, because international human rights are often descriptive, or even prescriptive, but they are rarely constitutional. Only national policies, state actions and programs, can implement and effectively protect human rights. Human rights require state support, because the norms contained in human rights instruments are voluntarily vague, due to the different constitutional traditions of the experts that negotiate them, and therefore require further national initiatives or adaptation, within both the legal and social contexts of a given country. Transposition and implementation require strong support from the state. At present, the European Court of Human Rights is the only example where international decisions have a direct effect within the legal order of the states that are party to the European Convention on Human Rights.[66]

The second set of limits of the justifications of the intervention is based on legal grounds, *stricto sensu*. The ECOWAS intervention violated Article 2 of the UN Charter, which opposes intervention in the domestic affairs of member states, the UN General Assembly resolutions on the non-use of force, the International Court of Justice interpretation of these resolutions, and Article 3 (2) of the former OAU Charter that reaffirmed the same prohibition. Furthermore, the ECOWAS intervention was not consistent with the African position on non-intervention at that time. There are other flaws in the justifications for the action carried out by the sub-regional organization as well.

Officially justified as a commitment to protect human rights, it remains to be proven that this reason was the primary impetus for ECOWAS intervention in Liberia. Humanitarian intervention, as its definition suggests, is *primarily* concerned with the protection of human rights. As stated earlier, the prevention of widespread deprivations of internationally recognized human rights should be the *sole* reason for humanitarian intervention.[67] If the legitimate reason for humanitarian intervention is the protection of human rights, justifying the ECOWAS intervention on that ground can raise legitimate doubts. None of the countries that initiated the intervention in Liberia was democratic. They were all military dictatorships or civilian autocracies. Babangida, like Doe, came to power through a military coup, and was one of the most violent dictator that Nigeria had ever had, with certainly one of the poorest human rights record in West Africa. Ghana's President Jerry Rawlings and Lansana Conté were basically dictators and, like the others, came to power through military coup. The president of Sierra Leone, Joseph Momoh, headed a one-party government, and the president of the fifth intervening state, Dauda Jawara, was the prince of Gambia since independence in 1965. In short, ideas of human rights, emancipation, equal opportunity, liberty, constitutionalism, democracy, and the rule of law have little resonance in the countries that initiated the intervention. One author describes the West African intervention as a coalition of dictatorial regimes whose objectives "were to resist the force of change which, in the sub-region, appeared to be represented by Charles Taylor's movement."[68]

Authorizing undemocratic regimes to promote the rule of law by intervening militarily in other countries is bad law that should be resisted because law is more praised when it is consonant with reason. It is unjust law because it violates the principle of equality, and the other name for it is tyranny. It is in fundamental contradiction with the legal and moral justifications for humanitarian intervention. The truth is that these justifications appeared to be inaccurate official history. It has been established beyond doubt that Côte d'Ivoire and Burkina Faso were sympathetic to Taylor's insurrection, while Nigeria, the intervention-initiator, was by contrast, supportive of Samuel Doe. Reading a leader's mind when it comes to humanitarian motives or to any human action is very difficult, but the personal relationships that have been documented between the president of Nigeria, Ibrahim Babangida, and the contested President Doe, were strong enough to assume that considerations other than purely humanitarian ones must have played a role. It has been documented that President Babangida provided Samuel Doe with assistance and supplied weapons and ammunitions to Monrovia during the AFL campaign in Nimba County.[69] Moral concepts are not applicable here.

Throughout the years, patronage and counter-support developed with disastrous consequences. Some member states of ECOWAS, in violation of the ethics of state responsibility, tolerated and even armed militias that operated from their territories. These interventions presented serious threats to the stability of all bordering states and clearly evolved into a sub-regional crisis. That support enabled the militias, for more than a decade, to carry out widespread rape of women, serious abuses against civilians and war crimes. Outsiders, including ECOWAS members, organized and facilitated the availability and the circulation of arms within and across borders, hence facilitating the formation of ill-disciplined militias, unaccountable mercenaries, who used the significant quantities of arms available to attack and massacre civilians. Is this disorder preferable to non-intervention? Is this really a good case to declare the current norms on non-intervention in a state's affairs obsolete? If the state is outdated who will implement, protect and enforce human rights? Is it really convincing to declare the current framework in need of revision because of the failure, incapacity or unwillingness of some states to perform their duties or to respect the norms of international society? The answer to this question is no.

Conversely, it is perplexing to agree to the justifications of the need to maintain regional security without taking into account the instability created by member states themselves. Collective security, simply understood, is a commitment to take common actions against those who threaten the territorial integrity or political independence of others.[70] In Liberia, ECOMOG became part of the problem, and it contributed to transforming the situation into a truly international threat. It is the first commandant of ECOMOG himself, Lieutenant General Arnold Quainoo, who openly admitted that ECOMOG troops used to sell arms to the faction leaders in Liberia.[71] This was not the only damage done. UN officials themselves reported that ECOMOG soldiers engaged in the systematic looting of small, easily transportable goods. The other rather cynical acronym for ECOMOG in the field was: "Every Conceivable Moving Object Gone."[72] The justification based on legitimate collective defense is important for our investigation, but if one looks more closely at the different aspects of the problem, one sees a legal enigma.

The third limit concerns the suitability of delegating military operations to regional organizations. Advocates of this "approach" argue that sub-regional organizations, when compared with other interveners, have political and military advantages.[73] It is said that contiguous states of a country in conflict suffer most from the destabilizing costs of war; that proximity presents political and military advantages for troops deployment and logistics. It is also declared that regional forces, because they understand the conflict better, are more politically acceptable by warring factions. By the same token, weak, inadequate, unqualified and ill-equipped regional forces can prolong the war, especially when they rely on external sources of aid, due to poverty. In Liberia, political acceptability has proven to be a conjecture, a simple speculation rather than empirical evidence. On the contrary, the evidence available supports the opposite argument. Armed groups never trusted the mediators. The mediation process in the Liberian crisis was marked by disordered and endless diplomatic maneuvers because of mutual suspicions among both militias and member states. Between 1990 and 1996, no fewer than thirteen cease-fires and agreements were signed, but none was implemented. These included (between June 1991 and June 1993) four peace accords and agreements signed in Yamoussoukro (Yamoussoukro I, II, III, and IV); the Cotonou and Akosombo agreements (between July 1993, and August 1994); and a series of peace agreements signed at Akosombo and Accra between September 1994 and August 1996. It became clear that these agreements were merely a means of jockeying for state power, and that the warlords were untruthful to each other and with those who were trying to mediate the conflict. Every agreement was quickly broken. These lessons were seemingly not taken into account in the new proposed approach.

Other practical problems exist as well. Despite proximity to the conflict, and a hypothetical political will, ECOWAS lack the capacity to take the level of action required in these conflicts. Proximity does not mean effectiveness. When the civil conflict broke out in Côte d'Ivoire, an ECOWAS member state, it took France three days to dispatch a peace keeping force compared with the three months it took the sub-regional organization to do so. Peace operations are expensive, and most African countries have moribund economies. The states lack resources and their armies require equipment and its maintenance.

Given all these limits (illegality of the intervention, political problems, practical difficulties, absence of clear direction) it is hard to accept the claims according to which the Liberian case has provided a new model for dealing with regional crises. Therefore, one may be circumspect to commentators who have declared that it was "an example for the rest of the world to follow."[74] The enthusiasm of weak and divided regional groupings undertaking poorly planned and hazardous interventions is irrational and should be resisted. If African leaders believe in human rights protection, they must do so through good governance and the democratic process. It requires enlightened leaders with political will.

METHODOLOGY

The approach of this book is a historical, normative and analytical one. It is inevitably interdisciplinary by the nature of the subject and integrates together three different traditions of scholarship: international public law, concepts of regionalism, and "African political science scholarship" with a focus on the state. International law dominates existing studies on humanitarian intervention and as ECOWAS, in part, based its justifications on that ground, these claims need to be discussed. The intervention initiated by the sub-regional organization has been presented as a new form of co-operation which will serve as an important mode of co-operation for conflict resolution, whether in Africa or elsewhere. Therefore, an examination of the sub-regional body's involvement during the conflict and its potential to carry future operations is needed. Finally, in Africa, the problem of humanitarian intervention goes beyond its objectives and considers action when the collapse of state authority threatens regional security. The interplay between pseudo-states and internal conflict requires another analysis. The best approach to preventing state disintegration and regional chaos is to insist on government legitimacy, but not to undertake or legitimize perilous interventions. In other words, military force is not the appropriate response to political problems.

No comprehensive work has yet been published on the Liberian war that focuses on the conflict from an objective normative approach that examines the most significant controversies in reference to the "anarchical society" of states. These core norms and values have been further investigated in a new, seminal work.[75] Most of the studies, limited in scope and covering the first years of the conflict, were written from the viewpoint of insiders, often military.[76] Additional studies have tried either to disentangle the complex sociological factors involved, including the mix of ethnicities, political allegiances, and the formation of militias,[77] or they have tried to comprehend the organizational methods and planning of peacekeeping operations.[78] More recent publications from the International Peace Academy's Occasional Paper

Series supported the sub-regional approach idea and claimed to offer solutions for the future.[79] The proponents of the sub-regional approach were certain that they had the solution. However, because the "model" was not based on hard facts and evidence, it was immediately proven to be wrong in the conflict in Côte d'Ivoire. Joseph E. Stiglitz has noted that when academics involved in policy recommendations they often become politicized and start to bend the evidence to fit the ideas of those in charge.[80] Trends and patterns do exist, but absolute predictability is impossible. Since none of these authors analyzed the conflict from an international society perspective, I believe that there is a need to approach the Liberian war in light of the post-1945 political and legal arrangements. As a normative and empirical question, this study will combine law, diplomacy, politics, and theory into a cohesive whole.

Chapter One consists of an analysis of the intervention in the context of the global normative framework contained in general principles of international law, and challenges the idea that the prerogatives of states derive from human rights and that wars in defense of human rights are *ipso facto* just.[81] It argues that a government that engages in substantial violations of human rights breaches the principle of *pacta sunt servanda,* but that the use of force to protect human rights is only legal when the violation represents a threat to international peace, as determined by the Security Council. A state that uses force in violation of international law contradicts the same *pacta sunt servanda* principle.

Chapter Two examines the limits of the justifications given by ECOWAS for intervening in Liberia in light of the fundamental contradiction between the rhetoric of human rights that were advanced as a legal basis for intervention and the relativist position adopted by those same states within the circles of the United Nations. ECOWAS actions in Liberia was in contradiction with the African position on non-interference. It further argues that the absence of a Security Council authorization, along with the poor human rights credentials of the countries that initiated the intervention, weaken the legal justifications.

Chapter Three claims once again that the ECOWAS intervention is a *nébuleuse.* While there is no substantive disagreement that the conflict presented a risk for the stability of the sub-region, it has been established that some ECOWAS member states have sponsored armed groups to destabilize other member states. Legal justifications and regional norms on regional security have to be confronted with the lack of neutrality and responsibility on the part of member states. A straightforward answer is impossible.

Chapter Four argues that because the interests of several of its members hampered ECOMOG, it was unable to achieve peace. It was only when the UN became involved that ECOWAS' action produced some measure of success. If one looks at what was achieved, the evidence cannot justify the decentralization of peace operations in favor of regional organizations. On the contrary, insufficiently and inexpertly planned interventions can do more harm than good.

Chapter Five discusses the regional approach proposed by ECOWAS and supported by the UN after the intervention. It argues that the approach is exceedingly simplistic. Liberia is in war for fifteen years, eight after the official end of the conflict and is completely devastated. At the level of institutional analysis, the approach has not added anything new to the incomplete mechanism that is supposed to exist between Chapter VIII of the UN and "regional arrangements or agencies." In fact, some developments that, on the surface, may appear new are in reality not that new at all.

Chapter Six argues that the conflict had its origins in the absence, or in the destruction, of the Liberian state between the April 1980 military coup and the beginning of the civil war in December 1989. The state never existed in Liberia since the very beginning. It will 'bring the state back in' as the *sine qua non* condition to address the root causes of these conflicts. Functioning states is the prerequisite to the effective promotion of human rights and good governance. National leaders will have to accept accountability for their failures and take responsibility for the destiny of their citizens.

Chapter One

Humanitarian Intervention versus Resilient Sovereignty

According to ECOWAS officials, the severe violations of human rights, mass starvation, displacement of the population and the risk of destruction of the Liberian state were a sufficient cause to justify the intervention.[1] This chapter argues that ECOWAS' intervention was contrary to the general principles of international law on the non-use of force. First, in international law there is no right to humanitarian intervention. Second, the UN Security Council did not authorize it. And finally, the countries that decided to intervene for the protection of human rights were denying human rights to their own citizens. The undemocratic nature of the Nigerian regime as well as the personal relationship between Babangida and Doe weaken the argument for intervention to defend human rights in this particular case.

ECOWAS AND THE NON-USE OF FORCE

The ECOWAS intervention violated well-established norms of international law. These are the principles of state sovereignty, domestic jurisdiction, non-intervention, peaceful settlement of disputes and the non-use of force. The UN Charter, general principles of customary international law, the General Assembly declarations, the OAU and the ECOWAS treaties all adopt the same position on the illegality of the use of force in inter-states relations. These documents will be examined here.

The United Nations was created as an organization based on the principle of equal and sovereign countries pursuing peaceful and friendly relations between states.[2] Under the UN Charter, states have agreed that they will refrain from the unlawful threat or use of force. Article 2 (4) of the UN

Charter provides that "[a]ll members shall refrain in their relations from the threat or use of force in the territorial integrity or political independence of any state or in other manner inconsistent with the Purposes of the United Nations." This article, which is the legal justification of the non-interventionist approach, is an essential principle of world politics. The prohibition and the attempt to control the use of force have been declared the cornerstone of the modern legal system.[3] Therefore, humanitarian intervention, or the use of force for the protection of human rights, conflicts with the legal principle of state sovereignty. The ECOWAS Standing Mediation Committee argued that when ECOWAS decided to intervene in Liberia, there was a total breakdown in government authority and therefore the regional organization had the right to use military force to protect the Liberians. Although the concern for human rights is legitimate, as Murphy notes, "[the] UN Charter, in the context of using military force is oriented to the preservation of order, not the protection of human rights."[4]

International lawyers have argued that the goal of humanitarian intervention is not to change the political organization or to compromise the territorial integrity of states, and therefore it is neither in contradiction with state sovereignty nor in violation of the UN Charter.[5] In Liberia, however, this argument is untenable. Indeed there was a clear interference in state sovereignty because ECOMOG did not call for the reinstallation of the Doe government. He was asked to step aside, and a national conference was organized after which Amos C. Sawyer was elected "Interim President." The initiative ran counter to the political independence of the Liberian people. Thus, this interpretation of the Charter does not constitute a valid reason for using force against a member state.

In the UN Charter, there are only two exceptions to the principle of nonintervention. Article 42 permits the use of armed force by the Security Council if the Council determines, under Article 39, the "existence of any threat to the peace, breach of the peace or act of aggression."[6] In addition, Article 51 preserves the "inherent right of individual or collective self-defense if an armed attack occurs against a Member of the United Nations, until the Security Council has taken measures necessary to maintain international peace and security." Therefore, as Michael Walzer maintains, "in the UN Charter only an aggression by a state against another justifies the use of armed force by the latter."[7] The Charter and the UN General Assembly consensus are identical. On December 1965, with 109 countries in favor, none against and none abstaining, the General Assembly adopted the Declaration on the Inadmissibility of Intervention in the Domestic Affairs of States and the Protection of Their Independence and Sovereignty, which stated:

> No State has the right to intervene, directly or indirectly, for any reason whatever, in the internal or external affairs of any other State. Consequently, armed intervention and all other forms of interference or attempted threats against the personality of the State or against its political, economic and cultural elements, are condemned . . . Every State has an inalienable right to choose its political, economic, social and cultural systems, without interference in any form by another State.

Similarly, the 1970 "Declaration on Principles of International Law concerning Friendly Relations and Co-operation among States in Accordance with the Charter of the United Nations" echoed the same non-interventionist approach:

> Every State has the duty to refrain from any forcible action, which deprives people . . . of their right to self-determination and freedom and independence. In their actions against, and resistance to, such forcible action in pursuit of the exercise of their right to self-determination, such peoples are entitled to seek and receive support in accordance with the purposes and the principles of the charter. [8]

These two crucial declarations have their origin in the role historically played by the General Assembly to advance the right of self-determination. ECOWAS representatives at the United Nations have vehemently defended this view. In 1987, the UN General Assembly adopted another document, the 'Declaration on the Enhancement of the Effectiveness of the Principle on Non-Use of Force in International Relations' where it exposes once again the principle of non-use of force and the principles laid down by Article 2 (4), to which the defense of human rights does not constitute a valid exception. [9] The very similarity of view between the UN General Assembly and the International Court of Justice on the importance of Article 2 (4) is apparent in the 1949 *Corfu Channel Case* [10] and the 1986 *Case Concerning Military and Paramilitary Activities In and Against Nicaragua.* [11] The Court's decisions have opposed to the exercise of armed force by one state against another, and its decisions are skeptical of the claims that the use of force to defend human rights is permissible. More importantly, the principle of non-use of force has been considered to be a rule of *jus cogens,* [12] that is, "a peremptory norm of international law, from which no subject of international law may derogate." In both cases, the Court declared intervention in the internal affairs of member states illegal.

In the *Corfu Channel Case,* the Court noted that regardless of the object of the action, Great Britain's intervention in the Albanian territory was a violation of Article 2 (4):

> The Court can only regard the alleged right of intervention as the manifestation of the policy of force, such as has, in the past, given rise to most serious abuses and such as cannot, whatever be the present defects of international organization, find a place of international law, intervention is still perhaps less admissible in the particular form it would take here; for, from the nature of things, it would be reserved for the most powerful States, and may easily lead to perverting the administration of international justice itself.[13]

In the previous cases, the Court was interpreting the general problem of non-intervention. Following the same jurisprudence, it noted this time, specifically with regard to humanitarian intervention, the following:

> The use of force could not be the appropriate method to monitor or ensure . . . respect for human rights. With regard to the steps actually taken, the protection of human rights, a strictly humanitarian objective, cannot be compatible with the mining of ports, the destruction of oil installations, or again with the training, arming or equipping of the contras. . . . [14]

These decisions confirm the importance of Article 2 (4) and must also be understood as the acceptance of the validity of the non-use of force in international affairs. The statements of the International Court of Justice and the General Assembly represent both customary international law and the cardinal principle of such law. The International Law Commission, in its work for the codification of the law of treaties, has expressed the same position regarding these rules,[15] and suggested that the prohibition of the use of force embodied in the Charter, has come to be recognized as a "universal norm," a "universally recognized principle of international law."[16]

Regional instruments also represent the view that the prohibition of intervention is universal international law. In Articles 2 and 3 of the then Charter of the Organization of African Unity, signed on May 25, 1963, African leaders placed a premium on state sovereignty, territorial integrity, and non-interference in members' internal affairs. African states solemnly declared that they would refrain from any intervention, direct or indirect, individual or collective, in the internal or external affairs within the domestic jurisdiction of another participating state. The ECOWAS Protocol on

Non-Aggression adopted in 1978 and the 1981 Protocol Relating to Mutual Assistance on Defense in 1981 were aimed at generating trust and confidence among the members to build their own collective security mechanism. However, several dispositions stipulate that the ECOWAS forces are not to intervene if a conflict remains "purely internal."[17] The intervention in Liberia was therefore in contradiction with Article 2 (4) and other provisions of customary law, which the great majority of international lawyers recognize as prohibiting the use of force.

Finally, there is not a single binding agreement that ECOWAS members could unhesitatingly advance as explicitly authorizing their action or justifying the use of force to protect human rights. More importantly, the fundamental principle of non-intervention in the internal affairs of a country would work, if it had been followed in the Liberian case. The most important problem that these states have faced was armed groups supported by member states. Specifically on that issue an essential UN General Assembly declaration proclaimed:

> The duty of a state to refrain from the promotion, encouragement or support, direct or indirect, of rebellious or secessionist activities within other states, under any pretext whatsoever, or any actions which seek to disrupt the unity or to undermine or subvert the political order of other states. . . . The duty of a state to refrain from the exploitation and the distortion of human rights issues as a means of interference in internal affairs of states, of exerting power on other states or creating disorder within and among states or groups of states.[18]

This cardinal declaration had anticipated that intervention in a sovereign country can bring about disorder and intensify human rights violations as was the case in Liberia. The declaration is a clear warning against the exploitation of the discourse of human rights to intervene in other countries.

In the Liberian war, states within the sub-region trained and provided backing to armed groups and rebels who destabilized the region. Such patronage is against the ethics of state responsibility. What is at issue in this situation is not the obsolescence of the current norms but their violation. ECOWAS members cannot, on the one hand, justify their intervention by invoking humanitarian motives, while some of its own members, on the other hand, were assisting and supporting the armed groups who were the source of human rights violations. There is no justification for assisting or training rebels to destabilize a neighboring country and one can argue that it could have been more difficult or even impossible for those groups to operate without the support of member states. Such sponsorship violates the territorial integrity of other states; it disputes the ethics of non-intervention, and is inconsistent with the purposes of the United Nations.

Not only is the argument based on the preservation of human rights questionable and suspect, but as we shall see in the following chapters, Nigeria did not give diplomacy a chance which constitutes a violation of the obligation imposed upon states to settle their international disputes by peaceful means in such a manner that international peace and security are not endangered. Military regimes, such as was the case in Nigeria, are always prompt to use force against any group that challenges them. Therefore, what is at stake is not the obsolescence of international norms but the fact that they have not been followed. Adherence to the principle of non-intervention and state responsibility might have prevented the humanitarian disaster. The fact that state intervention occurs does not constitute evidence that non-intervention is obsolete, nor does the evolution of the debate in the 1990s prove that there is a need to go beyond the current legal framework.

THE EVOLUTION OF THE DEBATE DURING THE 1990S AS AN INCONCLUSIVE LEGAL DOCTRINE

During the 1990s, there was a renewed interest in the doctrine of humanitarian intervention in the academic literature. It has been argued that sovereignty is anachronistic and irrelevant when applied to dictatorships and therefore needs to be replaced by "popular sovereignty vested in the individual citizens of a state."[19] The following section argues that what have changed are not the rules but their interpretation by scholars who have their personal and moral bias.

Today, non-intervention still remains the norm. If the motive of human rights can, under exceptional circumstances, challenge state sovereignty, this is limited to those cases of which the UN Security Council has determined that such violations constitute a threat to international peace and security. What has evolved is the extension of the "definition of the threat to peace" but that is not *per se* a legal basis for humanitarian intervention. If the Security Council, in order to intervene, is not referring explicitly to humanitarian intervention, but is debatably obliged to extend the notion of the threat to the peace in order to interfere, human rights so, have not superseded state sovereignty because in such situations the legal basis for intervention is not the violation of human rights that threaten a humane domestic society but violations of human rights that threaten the international order. These two situations are different. That justification will not be dealt with here since ECOWAS members did not raise it before the Security Council, which intervened *ex post facto*.

As has been said, the decline of sovereignty in international law and international relations is one of the main arguments of the proponents of humanitarian intervention.[20] Some authors have gone so far as to declare that "popular sovereignty had displaced the traditional notion of sovereignty as the critical new constitutive policy of international law."[21] According to that school of thought, which deviates from the confines of traditional international law, sovereignty should be adjusted so that human rights may be protected.[22] Michael Glennon maintains that respecting sovereignty is not pertinent where there is a state without a government (later referred to as "failed" or "collapsed state") because consent to intervene cannot be given.[23] In order to construct international law on a new foundation many arguments are presented. One of the most revolutionary among them argues that moral realities must lead to the revision of the legalist paradigm, so that any state capable of stopping injustices has a right to do so.[24] Human rights should take precedence over the norm of non-intervention. This idea is also supported by solidarists within the international society school. Although international society is a society of states, proponents of human solidarity argue that individuals have rights in international law and these rights can be enforced by other states in the name of solidarity and justice.[25]

Unfortunately, there is not yet in international law or politics an evolution that compellingly supports the idea that human and group rights must take precedence over states' rights. Nor is it at present a reality, because it is not humanitarian reasons but self-interest and ideology that drive the main actors of international politics. Great powers are increasingly reluctant to intervene where they do not have a direct national interest, and it is extremely difficult to convince public opinion of the necessity to send troops into countries with which these powers do not have close ties. One looks in vain for a moment of solidarity in which the protection of internationally recognized human rights of foreigners is more important than the national interest of the intervening countries. Wheeler's solidarism must be confronted with the reality, which is that for the great powers, human rights in other countries are not more important than their own national interests, and that these same powers are disengaging from states that hold no geo-strategic interest for them.

Statesmen acknowledge that intervention is selective and inconsistent. As Madeleine Albright puts it:

> The United States is sometimes criticized for inconsistency in its relations with governments that violate human rights, but a policy of consistent support does not require that we treat every country precisely the same. America has broad interests and responsibilities, and an approach that succeeds with Country A may well backfire with Country B.[26]

In the conduct of foreign policy, statesmen are generally careful, and human rights are "on the periphery of the periphery."[27] As the same author notes, "[t]aken in a foreign minister's baggage on a world tour, they might . . . spoil the whole trip."[28] When human rights conflict with other interests, leaders often focus not on the internal behavior of the regime, but on its external behavior because "human rights should not upset the good relations between two states."[29]

Nevertheless, the United Nations Secretaries General have adopted a more flexible view. In addition to the maintenance of international peace and security, the purpose of the UN is to promote the respect of human rights and fundamental freedoms. With this in mind, former Secretary General Javier Pérez de Cuéllar initiated the debate between state sovereignty and human rights before the General Assembly:

> It is now increasingly felt that the principle of non-interference with the essential domestic jurisdiction of states cannot be regarded as a protective barrier behind which human rights could be massively and systematically violated with impunity. The fact that, in diverse situations, the United Nations has not been able to prevent atrocities cannot be cited as an argument, legal or moral, against the necessary core action, especially where peace is threatened. Omissions or failures due to a variety of contingent circumstances do not constitute a precedent. The case for not impinging on the sovereignty, territorial integrity and political independence of States is by itself indubitably strong. But it would only be weakened if it were to carry the implication that sovereignty, even in this day and age, includes the right of mass slaughter or of launching systematic campaigns of decimation or forced exodus of civilian populations in the name of controlling civil strife or insurrection.[30]

This statement does not challenge the traditional construction placed on Article 2. It only calls for respect of human rights. It does not seek to weaken the principle of sovereignty but to reaffirm the necessity of sovereign states taking the matter seriously, which is the least that a Secretary General can suggest. In an address at the University of Bordeaux, France, Javier Pérez de Cuéllar restated the tension between the two sets of values (sovereignty and human rights). He suggested, in the following statement, not a limitation of sovereignty but a limitation of states' abuses of power:

> The right to intervene has been given renewed relevance by recent political events. We are clearly witnessing what is probably an irresistible shift in public attitudes toward the belief that the defense of the oppressed in

the name of morality should prevail over frontier and legal documents. Nevertheless, does it not call into question one of the cardinal principles of international law, one diametrically opposed to it, namely the obligation of non-interference in the internal affairs of states.[31]

This statement has been used and abused by authors who support intervention but nowhere did the Secretary General call for the abandonment of sovereignty. Indeed, he maintained that sovereignty is a *cardinal* principle of international law and that non-interference is *the* prevailing norm in international society. In recognition of this tension between the necessity of intervention under certain circumstances and the prevailing norm of international society, Javier Pérez de Cuéllar did not solve the "puzzle" which could not be settled by him, but called upon the international community to be sensitive to the importance of human rights.

This was also the position taken by his successor, Boutros Boutros-Ghali. The Egyptian diplomat restated the same tension as his predecessor, but once again, the position the Secretary General expressed did not propose to move beyond the concept of state sovereignty. "Respect for a state's fundamental sovereignty and integrity," Boutros Boutros-Ghali wrote, "is crucial to any common international progress." Nevertheless, he continued, "the time of absolute sovereignty has passed and it never matched with reality."[32] In fact, these dilemmas are at the center of the tensions running through the Charter: idealism and realism, human rights and sovereignty, but neither of the Secretaries General has suggested that human rights should take precedence. Such a possibility would diminish the norm of non-intervention. As Tom J. Farer has eloquently written:

> Anyone who considers with some measures of objectivity the Charter's normative logic, its allocation of coercive jurisdiction, its omissions, as well as the preferences manifested by most participants in the drafting process and their immediately subsequent behavior, cannot help concluding that the promotion of human rights ranked far below the protection of national sovereignty and the maintenance of peace as organizational goals.[33]

It is the current Secretary General, Kofi Annan, who has been the most vocal proponent of the move away from sovereignty. Addressing the same tension that his colleagues had struggled with, he called upon the international community to find a consensus and to search for unity around these basics. Before the General Assembly, the Secretary General articulated the debate in the following terms:

> If humanitarian intervention is, indeed, an unacceptable assault on sovereignty, how should we respond to a Rwanda, to a Srebrenica, to gross and systematic violations of human rights that affect every precept of our common humanity?[34]

The government of Canada, which since the earliest UN peacekeeping operations, has been committed to the issues of peace and security, responded to the Secretary General's remarks by announcing the establishment of an independent International Commission on Intervention and State Sovereignty (ICISS) in September 2000. The Commission comprised experienced individuals and prominent scholars and its composition was balanced between developed and developing countries in order to ensure the broad diversity of views on the subject. But before the commission had released its final work, the UN Secretary General expressed his own views in his Nobel Peace Prize lecture delivered in Oslo on December 10, 2001. His own sensibility, expressed in the form of just war doctrine, is clearly interventionist. He suggested moving away from a state-centered approach to the supremacy of the individual in world affairs and argued:

> The mission of the United Nations will be defined by a new, more profound awareness of the sanctity and dignity of every human life, regardless of race or religion. This will require us to look beyond the framework of States, and beneath the surface of nations or communities. We must focus, as never before, on improving the conditions of the individual men and women who give the state or nation its richness and character.[35]

This is a powerful statement in international politics for it clearly envisions that not states but the individuals are the essential subjects of global affairs. The point is not the legitimate concern that the UN Secretary General may have about human rights, but the implications of that position requires some examination.

Inevitably, a first observation is that this statement is in contradiction with a fundamental decision by the United Nations: The Vienna Declaration, which was adopted after the World Conference on Human Rights in June 1993. The Declaration and Programme of Action solemnly reaffirms:

> In accordance with the Declaration on Principles of International Law concerning Friendly Relations and cooperation Among States in accordance with the Charter of the United Nations, this shall not be construed as authorizing or encouraging any action which would dismember or impair, totally or in part, the territorial integrity or political unity of

sovereign and independent States conducting themselves in compliance with the principle of equal rights and self-determination of peoples . . . [36]

The conclusions of the ICISS report did not go as far as the Secretary General suggested either. Although the Commission's focus was to establish clearer rules, procedures and criteria for determining when, how and whether to intervene, and ensure that when an intervention occurs, it is carried out efficiently and effectively, it strongly emphasized that the primary responsibility for the protection of people lies with the state itself. It is beyond doubt that present history is witnessing the growth of a proactive diplomacy in favor of human rights. NGOs such as Amnesty International, the Minority Rights Group, Human Rights Watch, the International Committee of the Red Cross, the International League for Human Rights and the International Commission of Jurists, among others, regard themselves as promoters and defenders of human rights. Their experts gained more credibility over the past decades in proficiency and rigor in investigating human rights abuses and violations. They significantly contributed in shaping the agenda of the society of states by bringing new issues to the fore, such as women's and children's rights and environmental protection.

Amnesty International, for example, launched several initiatives on behalf of individuals. Letter-writing campaigns for political prisoners are an example of these actions. When NGOs are not satisfied they can condemn and speak out freely, but no means of implementation of human rights are available to them. When they have utilized all the means at their disposal, and when agitation fails, they turn to diplomacy to engage the state, whether on their own or through their home state governments. They can join the United Nations special sessions, which they often do, but they are not members of the organization and they do not vote on crucial issues. The United Nations is a collection of states, not a collection of NGOs or people. Finally, one may be skeptical of the Secretary General's suggestion to move beyond the state-centered approach because many non governmental organizations reflect only a tiny segment of the population of their member states. They largely represent only modernized countries and often have little independence from governments. The power of these "turbulent actors" in international politics remains limited. In general the society of states can support, promote, encourage, assist, and disseminate a culture of human rights through cooperative means, but not by using force (unless in the cases of transboundary effects). In such situations the society of states is not promoting human rights but preventing chaos and disorder. On closer inspection, most examples of transboundary effects presented as examples of a right to humanitarian intervention constitute an application of existing mechanisms, mainly those under Chapter VII of the UN Charter.

Nor can the position taken by the Secretary General at Oslo be justified under the Preamble to the Charter of the United Nations either. One can argue that the Preamble emphasizes that the objectives of the organization are to "save succeeding generations from the scourge of war" but also "to achieve international cooperation in . . . *promoting* and *encouraging* respect for human rights and fundamental freedoms . . ." However, the preamble is to be read together with Article 2(7), which states that "Nothing contained in the present Charter shall authorize the United Nations to intervene in matters which are essentially within the domestic jurisdiction of any state or shall require Members to submit such matters to settlement under the present Charter." As Seyom Brown notes, the promotion of universal respect for, and observation of, human rights and fundamental freedom contained in Article 55 is "a means of ensuring the conditions of stability and well-being necessary for peace and security."[37] There is no evidence in the UN documents that the leaders who constructed the United Nations had any intention of eroding the sovereignty of states in the name of human rights. It is not certain that this is the intention today.

Finally, at the practical level, the Secretary General's position expressed at Oslo is not convincing, either. There is no doubt that there is a plethora of actors who challenge the state. States are not the only actors in international politics, including in the domain of human rights. But, it is clearly an exaggeration to view the state as an "outdated concept," an "evaporating notion" a dying entity that has spent its "historical energy." This is not the reality in the domain of human rights because it is the state, and only the state, that can implement real protection of human rights. It is the state that negotiates and ratifies treaties, and it is the state that takes the appropriate measures at the national level. In a recent collection of essays, Michael Ignatieff correctly noted:

> It is utopian to look forward to an era beyond state sovereignty. Instead of regarding state sovereignty as an outdated principle, destined to pass away in the era of globalization, we need to appreciate the extent to which state sovereignty is the basis of order in the international system, and that national constitutional regimes represent the best guarantees of human rights.[38]

The UN Charter recommends that member states cooperate with the UN in the promotion of human rights and fundamental freedoms, and the organization has indeed taken massive efforts to codify and define a corpus of international human rights. Over the years, it has also clarified the scope of member states' obligation to "promote" human rights in numerous international instruments. When a state is engaged in gross violations of internationally recognized human rights, it clearly violates the UN Charter. Should this happen, the UN has at its disposal procedures to review allegations of violations and resolutions calling on a state to stop such violations, but the procedures themselves protect the sovereignty of the state. The extent to which it allows the use of force is subject to the determination of a threat to international peace. The last century has demonstrated that war and chaos often breed massive violations of human rights. Recent internal conflicts prove that abuses are higher in the absence of a functioning state. Therefore, the debate should not seek to reduce the relevance of the state on matters pertinent to human rights but to assert its indispensability in effectively protecting human rights by observing the body of international human rights law to which it has subscribed.

Chapter Two
Bold Rhetoric Ambivalent Action

At the end of the 1980s, public statements that promised the promotion of human rights and democratic norms of governance followed the debate on democratization in Africa. This chapter will look at these justifications, which, in large part, appear to be rhetoric that cannot constitute a legal basis for intervening in a sovereign country. It will then analyze the African states' position on intervention. At the United Nations, these states defended the right to political independence and the respect of cultural relativism, which is in contradiction with the intervention in Liberia. Furthermore, although the Security Council became more flexible in defining threats to international peace, what, in the case of ECOWAS has been called *ex post facto* authorization remains uncertain. The chapter argues that action based on a Security Council authorization is preferable to unilateral intervention that is more bluntly based on power.

RHETORIC OR SHIFT IN THE AFRICAN POSITION ON NON-INTERVENTION?

It has been argued that after an absolute defense of state sovereignty in the first decades of independence, African leaders are moving toward the idea that the principle of non-intervention does not confer absolute immunity on any government to commit monumental crimes.[1] In an address to his fellow heads of states, Nelson Mandela observed that the clause of domestic jurisdiction cannot justify egregious human rights violations:

> Africa has a right and a duty to intervene to root out tyranny . . . we must all accept that we cannot abuse the concept of national sovereignty to deny the rest of the continent the right and the duty to intervene

when, behind those sovereign boundaries, people are being slaughtered to protect tyranny.[2]

Other African leaders urged their fellows to accept limitations of their sovereignty to protect human rights and develop greater security. The president of Gambia, then chairman of ECOWAS, stated that "ECOMOG was not an invasion force but its task was strictly humanitarian, helping civilians caught in the civil war get relief supplies."[3] This was also the position adopted by Nigeria's president who claimed that the presence of ECOMOG was due to "the horrible events, which led to massive destruction of property and the massacre of innocent civilians."[4] Other African leaders, such as Museveni of Uganda and Mugabe of Zimbabwe, paid tribute to the role of ECOMOG and echoed the sentiments that non-interference should not be taken to mean indifference to human rights.

Former Secretary General of the OAU, Salim Ahmed Salim, has also voiced such a view at the London Africa Centre's annual lecture in October 1990. According to the Tanzanian diplomat, the OAU Charter cannot be interpreted to mean ignoring massive human rights violations by member states:

> The Charter was created to preserve human dignity, and the rights of the African. You cannot use a clause of the Charter to oppress the African and say that you are implementing the OAU Charter. What has happened is that people have interpreted the Charter as if to mean that what happens in the next house is not one's concern. This does not accord with the reality of the world.[5]

With reference to the legality of the intervention in Liberia, Salim noted that it would have been most desirable to have an agreement of all parties to the conflict. Despite the lack of convergence, he supported the intervention:

> To argue that there was no legal base for any intervention in Liberia is surprising. Should the countries in West Africa, should Africa just leave the Liberians to fight each other? Will that be more legitimate? Will that be more understandable?[6]

The former Secretary General has been active in introducing retaliatory measures against unconstitutional changes of government in Africa. Solemnly, military regimes are prevented from attending continental summits as the idea of "sovereignty as responsibility" is taking root in African diplomacy.[7] But with reference to the intervention in Liberia, the situation is different: an organization can define the conditions of membership; in Liberia the issue was the use of armed force in a sovereign country. The point that Salim A. Salim makes (to let the Liberians fight is not understandable) is not a legal argument. There is no dispute that substantive violations of human rights have occurred in Liberia. Bodies littered the capital; there was mass starvation, widespread disease, and, according to one writer, the death toll reached near genocidal-proportions.[8] At the Ministerial Meeting of the ECOWAS Standing Mediation Committee, no one doubted the extreme suffering of the people of Liberia.[9] Analysts confirmed that armed groups had installed a reign of terror, destroyed houses and deprived the local population of food, holding people hostage and inflicting on them treatment contrary to all standards of civilized behavior.[10] In fact, the government could not govern and there was no state, but a profound anarchy and a total breakdown of law and order.[11]

The decision of the heads of states and governments of ECOWAS to send troops after their meeting in Banjul in August 1990 can be justified as a matter of self-help. Although non-intervention is the norm, in the situation of state desperation, when foreigners are the only ones who can end the atrocities and mass killings, inaction can be unjustifiable. Otherwise the international society of states faces the risk of blame for moral indifference. Therefore, the decision of African leaders to protect the lives of innocent people is, to use Salim's word, understandable, and indeed legitimate. So are, given the anarchic state of affairs in Liberia, the efforts to try to restore order, the practical measures to alleviate human suffering, to provide a buffer zone, to perform relief work, and to distribute food and medicines.[12] These actions are part of humanitarian assistance, and victims have rights to protection as stipulated in the Geneva Conventions and Protocols on International and Internal armed conflicts.[13] These norms protect what are referred to as victims *hors combat*. But there is a tendency to confuse humanitarian assistance and humanitarian intervention. The objectives of humanitarian assistance are to gain access to the victims especially when they are suffering undue hardship owing to the lack of the supplies essential for their survival. The main body of law on which the right to assistance is based is the 1949 Geneva Conventions and the two additional Protocols of 1977. Originally, the Geneva conventions related solely to international armed conflict, but Protocol II broadened the protection as to include non-international armed conflicts. [14]

As for the norms contained in the UN Charter they have not changed since their adoption. If the evolution of international human rights law and the Charter have had any revolutionary effect on the international legal system, it is through interpretation and even more so through increasing doctrinal manipulation. Fernando Tesòn is among those advocates of the right of humanitarian intervention who argue that the individual lies at the center of international law and that states derive their legitimacy from the will of the people. According to that view, sovereignty is not an inherent right of states but, rather, derives from individual rights. Therefore, when sovereignty conflicts with human rights, the latter must prevail:

> The human rights imperative underlies the concepts of state and government and the precepts that are designed to protect them, most prominently Article 2 (4). The rights of states recognized by international law are meaningful only on the assumption that those states minimally observe individual rights. The United Nations purpose of promoting and protecting human rights found in Article 1 (3), and by reference in Article 2 (4) as a qualifying clause to the prohibition of war, has a necessary primacy over the respect for state sovereignty. Force used in defense of fundamental human rights is therefore not a use of force inconsistent with the purposes of the United Nations. [15]

This is debatable. As noted earlier, there is no evidence that in the UN Charter the protection of human rights prevails over state sovereignty. On the contrary, the principle contained in Article 2 (4) is the cornerstone of the Charter. His interpretation does not conform to international law, but represents an attempt to refashion international law according to the author's preference or, to emerging ethical standards of international behavior, which in a pluralistic world would be impossible to determine and enforce. If human rights take precedence in a world where values differ and many regimes are barbaric, interstate relations are at risk. The author does not seem to take that point into account.

This work is critical of intervention but I am not arguing against the values and the importance of human rights standards. Human rights is a subject of legitimate concern for everybody. In a situation such as Liberia's, where order broke down, the state is incapable of acting to protect the masses of citizens and a whole population is in danger, inaction is difficult to justify. But from a purely legal perspective, intervention is not justified whenever and wherever human rights are violated. Human rights abuses *per se* are not a legal ground for armed intervention. As Sean D. Murphy notes, "In the UN Charter, there is no explicit provision that authorizes the international organization or a group of states to use force to enforce human rights."[16] Once again, the wording of the Charter is prudential. What it does is to affirm the importance of human rights, the commitment of the organization to human rights protection and invite states to "encourage" "promote" and "assist" in the realization of human rights. In other words, the role of the society of states is not to enforce human rights in any place by using force, but to cooperate in order to promote adherence to a culture of, and respect for human rights.

It is that approach that is captured in the Preamble to the UN Charter. It emphasizes cooperation rather than the use of force. The word cooperation is emphasized in almost all articles dealing with human rights. According to Article 1 (3), "the purposes of the United Nations are to achieve international *cooperation* in solving international problems and in *promoting* and *encouraging* respect for human rights and for fundamental freedom for all without distinction as to race, sex, language or religion." Under Articles 55 and 56, members are committed "to take joint and separate action in *cooperation* with the organization for the promotion of the equal rights of people . . . including universal respect for an observance of human rights."

These dispositions do not carry more weight than Article 2 which clearly restrains states from the threat or use of force against the 'territorial integrity or political independence' of any state, in "matters that are essentially within the domestic jurisdiction of any state." If these dispositions conflict, respect for sovereignty must prevail. Two arguments in the UN Charter support that view. The first one is historical. With the different political traditions within the countries that composed the United Nations, an agreement on a clear definition of human rights would have been impossible. Another argument that can be put forward is that at the time, it would have been unthinkable to have the drafters accept the idea of human rights superseding state sovereignty because in 1945, the violators of human rights were the UN Security Council permanent members. Each of them had troublesome records on human rights violations: the gulag, China, racism in the United States, colonialism and crime against humanity by France and Great Britain in their colonies. For these reasons it is difficult to accept the view that the great powers could have envisioned the permissibility of the use of force to defend human rights.

At the institutional level, the sharing of responsibilities between the Security Council and the other organs reinforces that doubt. The Security Council is not in charge of human rights (except when their violations threaten international peace and security); the General Assembly is. This latter organ studies and makes recommendations for the purpose of "promoting international co-operation in political field and encouraging the progressive development of international law and its codification."[17] The General Assembly and the Economic and Social Council are expressly in charge of human rights, while the Security Council is not. Following the Vienna Declaration and Programme of Action and General Assembly Resolution 48/141 of 20 December 1993, the Centre for Human Rights and the Office of the United Nations High Commissioner for Human Rights merge into a single Office of the United Nations High Commissioner for Human Rights as of 15 September with the objectives of promoting international cooperation for human rights; providing education, information, advisory services and technical assistance in the field of human rights; supporting human rights organs and treaty monitoring bodies, promoting universal ratification and implementation of international standards, among others.

If one accepts that the Security Council is the most important UN institution, one cannot argue that human rights are on the same level as state sovereignty, the non-use of force, or peace and security, which is the *domaine réservé* of the Security Council. As an international lawyer notes, if human rights were in the same rank as peace and security, the Security Council would not leave it in declaratory form, and under the jurisdiction of other declaratory organs.[18] The promotion of human rights and democracy cannot justify the use of force.[19] When states violate international conventions on human rights, that protection takes the form of such arrangements as provided for in the conventions themselves,[20] and none of these includes the use of force as a means of protecting or monitoring human rights. Therefore, the official position adopted by ECOWAS leaders as well as the interpretation of human rights clauses in the UN Charter do not provide a legal justification for the intervention in Liberia, especially when at the same time intervention for humanitarian or other motives was not welcomed in the continent.

THE AFRICAN POSITION ON NON-INTERVENTION

Africa's traditional perspective on intervention is based on the continent's past experience with colonization. The degrading history of colonization still influences African thinking on that subject. European powers presented their intrusions in Africa as a humanitarian mission that sought to bring the benefits of Christianity and Western civilization to what they termed "barbarous peoples." After the process of decolonization, states were granted the right to freely decide their internal affairs and because of the past colonial experience, there is in Africa an almost allergic reaction to intervention and "trusteeship," even in failing states. Weak states view intervention as a neo-colonialist action, which continues to scar many countries and are attached to their newly acquired rights. Generally speaking, Third World countries have argued that different civilizations and traditions have different routes of achieving political development, and in matters relating to solving problems internal to another culture, foreigners are viewed as incompetent. With regard to human rights the UN adopted the same approach. Evidence of such an approach can be found in the works of the Commission on Human Rights under the auspices of the United Nations Economic and Social Council in 1986. The Commission, whose role was to strengthen the United Nations' general understanding of the issues of human rights, started its task by selecting "basic works on human rights for use by the United Nations information centers."[21] Among the three books chosen there was one with a title that speaks for itself: *Human Rights: Cultural and Ideological Perspectives*, published in 1979 and authored by Adamantia Pollis and Peter Schwab. It was one of the pioneering works on cultural relativism investigating "the extent to which the doctrines of human rights . . . embodied in the Universal Declaration of Human Rights . . . may not be relevant to societies with a non-Western cultural tradition or a socialist ideology."[22]

The Commission was concerned with giving the same importance to Third World countries that emphasize the rights of the group, economic subsistence and to Western perceptions of human rights as more individual.[23] Each approach was entitled to a fair hearing. Simply put, most Third World countries define human rights differently than the West. Human rights principles in the South require that the state shall guarantee economic, social and cultural rights, and provide for better education. Western political rights based on the writings of philosophers such as Grotius, Locke, Montesquieu, and Rousseau, among others, were peripheral to these concerns.[24] The United Nations accepted such diversity among its member states and instituted it in the form of law guaranteed by the principle of non-intervention and the right to self-determination.

African leaders have always defended the view that intervention was an infraction to their sovereignty and that they have the right to rule their own domains. It is why they are independent. Non-intervention has always been important to African states because it is a protection for them against stronger states. The European justifications of African colonization, through arguments of humanitarian mission, continue to make Africans inherently wary and circumspect of external discourses of altruism, philanthropy or humanitarian protection. Therefore they are attached to all international rights that recognize and protect their sovereignty, such as the legal right of states contained in the UN Charter, to freely determine their political institutions.[25]

Not only is humanitarian intervention viewed with suspicion, but it is also seen as paternalistic. Adam Roberts rightly notes that "there is a germ of paternalism behind the doctrine of humanitarian intervention, and paternalism conjures up memories of imperialism, racism and humiliation in these countries."[26] There is no room for paternalism in international politics. The term, at the very best, posits inequality. It assumes that adults in other countries are like young children, incapable and incompetent. Paternalists suppose that they can make better judgment than the people for whom they act. Applied to states, paternalism justifies interference in a state against the will of that state for the reason that its internal affairs will be better. Paternalism is a violation of the equal sovereignty of states.

Paternalism is not pure because it assumes that people in some hemisphere are incompetent and weak. The most important good for a state is to be respected as an independent agent, having the right to make its own decisions. Peoples' beliefs must be valued, because determining what benefits them depends on one's understanding of the good. We are reminded by Mill that a man's mode of determining his personal existence is optimal not because it is the best in itself, but because it is his own mode.[27] Paternalism is a normative issue as well. Because there is no burden of proof attached to paternalism, states are not permitted to act for others against their wishes or in any way that can limit their liberty and their independence. Paternalistic interference is the opposite of respect for the rational agency of others.

ECOWAS members vehemently echoed that view at the United Nations as illustrated in the statement of Ghana's representative:

> The group of 77 is slightly worried that some . . . may not be sensitive to certain pleas for an abiding respect for the sovereignty of nations. Our concerns stems from our historical past, when many of us, as colonial subjects, had no rights. The respect for sovereignty which the United Nations system enjoys is not an idle stipulation that can be rejected in the name of even the noblest gestures . . . An essential attribute of that sovereignty is the principle of consent, one of the cornerstones in the democratic ideal itself. [28]

This is nebulous. It is surprising that at the same time when ECOWAS members were in Liberia in the name of human rights, they opposed the principle of intervention. It seems that non-intervention is more in conformity with the African position, as these same states persistently supported it, during the same period, in various preparatory meetings of the World Conference on Human Rights in Vienna in June 1993. They have demanded the UN to take into consideration "the significance of regional and national particularities and the various historical, cultural and religious backgrounds."[29]

African leaders have endorsed the idea that rules about morality vary from one place to another and that the way to understand that heterogeneity is to place it in context. There is no universal morality because the history of the world is diverse and plural, and "human rights can only possess meaning within concrete societies."[30] For those reasons, they have supported the position expressed by the Commission on Human Rights on cultural diversity, and its representatives adopted a cultural relativist perspective. After the imperial disasters in the continent it was hard for an African to believe in the humanitarian reasons advanced by a Western country. Human rights are viewed as an attempt to extend the sphere of liberal values to social contexts in which those values do not hold and to force Western notions on foreigners, which is a form of moral imperialism.[31] Therefore, the interpretation based on the protection of human rights is in contradiction with the African position that is opposed to intervention, especially without the authorization of the Security Council.

THE ILLEGALITY OF A NON-AUTHORIZED INTERVENTION

ECOWAS undertook its intervention without specific authorization of the UN Security Council. The organization clearly ignored Article 52 of the Charter which states that: "Nothing in the present Charter precludes the existence of regional arrangements or agencies dealing with matters relating to the maintenance of international peace and security as are appropriate for regional action, provided that such arrangements and agencies and their activities are consistent with the Purposes and Principles of the United Nations." But, under Article 53 no enforcement action may be taken by regional organizations without an authorization of the Security Council,[32] which must be kept informed of activities pursued under regional arrangements or agencies for the maintenance of peace and security.[33]

The Charter does not make clear whether regional arrangements or agencies under Article 52 (1) must have been created for the purpose of dealing with matters relating to the maintenance of international peace and security.[34] ECOWAS, as its name indicates, was initially designed as a sub-regional integration organization in pursuit of economic and social aims: "It shall be the aim of the community to promote co-operation and development in all fields of economic activity particularly in the fields of industry, transport, telecommunications . . . and in social and cultural matters for the purpose of raising the standards of living of its peoples . . ."[35] Without belaboring the issue, it can be said that ECOWAS acted as a regional agency or government in the sense of Article 52 of the UN Charter.[36] But although ECOWAS was qualified as an organization under Article 52 (1), an intervention not authorized by the Security Council is illegal because the legal basis of intervention under these dispositions is not the doctrine of humanitarian intervention but the maintenance of international peace and security. ECOWAS violated an important requirement of Article 52 which is the obligation to first explore peaceful solutions because the use of force is not an automatic option under 52 or under Chapter VII, since otherwise it would have ruined the whole edifice of Chapter VI.[37] Since neither a general right nor a clear legal basis for humanitarian intervention exist; such action will only be legal or permissible when the Security Council decides that massive violation of human rights falls under the definition of a threat to international peace and security. Without that determination by the Security Council, a regional organization cannot initiate the action. It can only conduct a military operation with the blessing of the Security Council, accrediting the regional organization to act on behalf of the international community. Since the regional organization cannot determine on its own that international peace and security are threatened, authorization is needed.[38] This requires the UN Security Council authorization to determine if such a purpose is justified.

The same legal questions have been raised in the aftermath of the Kosovo crisis and of NATO's bombing campaign against Serbia. In light of the large number of justifications, some measure of prudence is needed. The decentralization of peace operations under Chapter VIII of the Charter should not be in contradiction with a global, as opposed to a regional, approach to the issues of international peace and security. The Charter is unhesitatingly clear on that issue: regional bodies need the authorization of the Security Council before launching an intervention under Chapter VIII. Otherwise, regional bodies can weaken the role of the Security Council. When the use of military force is necessary, regional organizations must act in a manner compatible with the primary responsibility of the UN for international peace and security. After the controversial interventions of ECOWAS in Liberia and Sierra Leone and of NATO action in Kosovo, it has been argued that the Security Council endorsed these actions *ex post facto*. The Commission on State Sovereignty and Intervention argues that this type of action is an implicit, retroactive rendering of legality to the international action:

> One view that has some currency is the *ex post facto* authorization, of the kind that has occurred for the African regional instances [i.e., Liberia and Sierra Leone], might conceivably have been obtained in the Kosovo and in the Rwanda cases, and may offer a way out of the dilemma should any case occur again in the future.[39]

This interpretation is uncertain, almost incorrect, because rules that have had a fixed interpretation are to be altered as little as possible.[40] The solution is not constructing hazardous justifications (implicit or retroactive endorsement) but it is getting the Security Council to exercise its responsibility, and this is a matter of primary importance. If a situation constitutes a threat to international peace, it necessitates an unambiguous determination and effective action by the Security Council. Retroactive authorization (*ex post facto*) does not exist under chapters VII and VIII. If the option of an *ex post facto* authorization is recognized, it means that states can do whatever they want, and then retroactively receive the Security Council's approval. If such possibility is recognized, there is no compelling need to seek prior authorization. In law, if authorization is required it is always prior to the action. Retroactive law, which consists "in the application of a new rule of law to an act which was completed before the rule was promulgated,"[41] has no juridical status under the Charter. The Vienna Convention on the law of treaties concluded on 23 May 1969 and in force since 27 January 1980 includes a clause on the non-retroactivity of treaties.[42] The UN Charter does not refer to the notion; therefore there is no legal basis in support of this position, at least in this case. International law should not be manipulated for the convenience of particular situations.

Law needs to be clear; otherwise its credibility is undermined and that certainty is at risk when such interpretation develops and gains acceptance. As French lawyers say, *Toute exception non surveillée tend à prendre la place du principe*. Law cannot be at the mercy of circumstances. It cannot be tailored to fit flawed justifications, especially when it comes to setting precedents and indeed, as with the issue of intervention, a highly important precedent. Moreover, this trend is dangerous because what is at stake is peace and stability in the world. *Ex post facto* authorization presents legal incertitude, may engender insecurity, and jeopardize order, as was the case in Liberia, and as may be the case when countries manipulate that loophole. Supported by the rhetoric of human rights, that pretext may destabilize an enemy regime or serve to settle accounts. In these situations an impartial party is necessary. With countries that have demonstrated hostility toward each other, abundant caution does no harm. Caution requires that the action be approved and be supported unanimously by the Security Council, not *ex post facto* but prior to the intervention. It requires the Security Council to respect the principles that govern the Charter and to fulfill its role by taking action promptly in cases where it should, and Liberia was among these. Intervention is already an enigma, a very complex issue and by fulfilling its role, the Security Council can alleviate some of the uncertainties surrounding its use.

Several sources have argued that the Security Council did not consider the Liberian situation as a serious threat to general international peace and security because it was preoccupied by the Gulf War.[43] If it is true, this politics of double standards contributes to create a situation that makes other small states and non Security Council members feel that the Security Council is not representative of the global community. On Liberia, it issued only a vague statement:

> The members of the Security Council take note of the final communiqué
> of the first extra-ordinary session of the Heads of State and Government

of the Economic Community of West African States (ECOWAS) issued in Bamako, Mali, on 28 November 1990. The Members of the Security Council commend the efforts made by the ECOWAS Heads of State and Government to promote peace and normalcy in Liberia. The members of the Security Council call upon the parties to the conflict in Liberia to respect the cease-fire agreement, which they have signed, and to co-operate fully with the ECOWAS to restore peace and normalcy in Liberia.

Although the statement does not specifically refer to retroactive authorization, one can argue that the Security Council gave its support to the ECOWAS intervention, as appears in a more evident fashion in the following statement of the Secretary General:

Liberia continues to represent an example of systematic and effective cooperation between the United Nations and regional organizations, as envisaged in Chapter VIII of the Charter. The role of the United Nations has been a supportive one. Closest contact and consultation have been maintained with ECOWAS, which will continue to play the central role.[44]

Implicit endorsement is not sufficient. If the Security Council wants an international order based on respect for the rule of law, it should uphold the principles of the Charter and act adequately when the situation requires it. The Security Council failed its responsibility under the Charter. Other ECOWAS countries decided to take the lead, but one cannot evaluate the rationale put forth without examining the human rights credentials of the intervening countries.

AN ERROR OF LAW INJURES

Humanitarian intervention undertaken by undemocratic countries is unjust law and poor policy. Many interventions are described as humanitarian but few, in fact, are. It was Nigeria that took the diplomatic offensive by seeking ECOWAS support for the deployment of a force in which, according to one author, it provided seventy five percent of the troops and ninety five percent of the funding.[45] Nigeria's justifications should be analyzed together with the role it aspired to play within the region, as well as the personal relationship said to have existed between the presidents of both countries. Given Nigeria's poor record on human rights, democracy and governance, its intervention was a manifestation of power. Force without justice is tyranny.

Several theories of international relations recognize the existence of as well as the need for hegemony.[46] But in Liberia the hegemon only used its influence to pursue its own agenda. Historically, Nigeria appointed itself as the protector of the other states against France's neocolonialism in West Africa. Former Nigerian President, Shehu Shagari (1979–83) described Nigeria's role in West Africa in the following terms: "Just as President Monroe proclaimed the American hemisphere free from the military incursions of Europeans' empire builders and adventurers, so also do we . . . in Nigeria and in Africa insist that African affairs be left to Africa to settle."[47] This statement echoed in its tone Nigeria's first president, Nnamdi Azikiwe, who spoke of the "historic and manifest destiny of Nigeria on the African continent."[48] The same rhetoric about Nigeria's historical mission has been widely reaffirmed by its diplomats and the following statement is attributed to a Nigerian ambassador: "Africa is Nigeria's natural sphere of influence. To shirk this manifest destiny is not to heed the logic of history."[49] A sphere of influence, however, is not an internationally recognized legal category. The point of emphasis is how Nigerians saw their role in the sub-region. It has been concerned mainly with countering French presence in West Africa. Nigeria has perceived France as a major threat to the realization of its strategic and geopolitical goals. The creation of ECOWAS, led by Nigeria itself, was a reaction to the French-sponsored formation of the *Communauté Economique de l'Afrique de l'Ouest (CEAO)* which was comprised of the French-speaking countries of Bénin, Burkina Faso, Côte d'Ivoire, Mali, Niger, Sénégal and Togo and become *l'Union Economique et Monétaire Ouest Africaine* in January 1994 with these members.[50]

Although President Ibrahim Babangida said that he was extremely pained by the human catastrophe inflicted on the Liberian population, [51] the decision to lead the intervention may have had other motivations, especially in light of Nigeria's longstanding aspirations to be the *gendarme* in West Africa. Liberia was Nigeria's test of leadership capabilities, an example of what it could accomplish as a regional power. It was Babangida's test and opportunity to enter history by fulfilling the aspirations of his predecessors. Without denying the possible concern for the suffering of Liberians, the intervention can be interpreted one way or another. President Babangida, who initiated the intervention, had a very close relationship with President Samuel Doe.[52] In that vein, Amadu Sesay argues that the operation in Liberia was a sort of "camaraderie rescue," a matter of help to a friend whose regime "was in mortal danger of collapse."[53] According to many, the Nigerian-led intervention was intended to safeguard a close friend of the President who was at the point of losing the war:

> Our government's failure to make arrangements to evacuate stranded
> Nigerians from Liberia is counted as evidence of Nigeria's support for
> Doe's regime. Nigeria refused to evacuate her citizens to create a façade
> of stability in Liberia. Government did not want to give the impression
> that Doe had lost control of the situation, which could have a negative
> psychological effect on the war effort.[54]

Liberians interviewed for this work held the same view. It is impossible to
read the mind of a leader, and difficult to rationalize with certainty what
his real motivations are, but these reservations need to be taken into consideration. The fact that, not only Nigeria, but also the other intervening
countries, Gambia, Ghana, Guinea, and Sierra Leone, had at a time established a network of official and unofficial relations with Babangida constitutes another reason to be skeptical. These same countries have benefited
from Nigeria's economic, financial, technical, and military assistance in the
years before the war, and have established a sort of dependency toward
Nigeria and several other connections in which personal relationships
between leaders played their part.[55]

Finally when Nigeria intervened in Liberia for the restoration of
human rights, Nigeria was a tyranny *par excellence*. A scholar described
Nigeria as a "form of military autocracy for most of the 1990s, which
abandoned the consensual format of the military governments of the 1970s
and 1980s in favor of personalized military power marked by state violence."[56] This is not the place to study the nature of the Nigerian regime;
many authors have already addressed this subject.[57] One of the premises of
humanitarian intervention is to defend human rights when a government
massively violates internationally agreed standards. But, ironically,
Babangida was one of the harshest dictators Nigeria ever had.[58] He lacked
any concern for human rights violations against his own citizens, who
need and deserve protection as much as Liberians. While pretending to
bring human rights to Liberia, political violence, tyranny, despotism and
torture escalated as major politicians were arrested in Nigeria. Human
Rights Watch, Amnesty International, other NGOs, the Nigerian press,
and civil liberties organizations recorded secret trials, the use of the state
police to kill opponents, secret deaths, and harassment of journalists, abusive detentions, and kidnappings in Nigeria. An outlaw state cannot and
should not be the guarantor of international legitimacy. Humanitarian
intervention undertaken by such a regime would discredit, not reinforce
support for intervention. Pretending to bring democracy and human rights
to the neighbor while denying it at home is a form of hypocrisy and the
'international community' should not give *carte blanche* to such a regime

to intervene, nor retroactively endorse its intervention. Not only order but also justice is in danger in these situations.

Finally, I have argued that on the problem of intervention, the African position was close to that of Asian, Latin American and other developing nations in opposing universal recognition of any doctrine that may authorize any one country or group of countries to intervene on an allegedly humanitarian basis. The countries that intervened in Liberia failed to provide convincing justifications that the protection of Liberian rights was the primary motives of the intervention, especially when none of them was democratic. It has been said that the Security Council's inaction frustrated ECOWAS leaders but two violations do not reconcile the situation. Intervention in a state's internal affairs by using force, without the Security Council's authorization is still illegal. A detached analysis of the justifications based on the need to protect regional security reveals other incoherencies as we will see in the next chapter.

Chapter Three
Regional Security and Machinations

This chapter analyses the justifications of the intervention from the perspective of regional security. The neighbouring countries of Sierra Leone and Guinea were facing many risks of instability such as the presence of armed groups and rebels, the alarming proliferation of light weapons, the flux of refugees and displaced persons. Some regional norms and general principles of international law authorize intervention under these circumstances. However, the problem of regional security was not raised at the beginning of the intervention because when ECOMOG decided to intervene, the conflict was internal, albeit with some regional repercussions in the form of refugees and displaced people. The legal enigma is not so much the absence of legal grounds, but rather the fact that some ECOWAS members themselves had largely sponsored the armed groups that were destabilizing the sub-region. Therefore, a strict legal interpretation of international law and regional treaties is insufficient to explain the situation.

THE EXISTENCE OF A THREAT TO REGIONAL SECURITY AND ORDER

The term "internal conflict" is misleading in many conflicts. The Liberian war was not wholly internal, because it had the potential, and indeed destabilized Sierra Leone and Guinea as well as the border areas of the three countries, due to the movement of refugees, displaced persons, armed groups and militias, and the proliferation of arms. The movement of people and arms affected these states and threatened regional security because most African conflicts spill over national borders and create the risk of destabilizing already weak economies. As the war continued, the situation became increasingly confused as, often with outside support, new groups of rebels appeared and existing groups fragmented.[1]

The situation was further complicated by the widespread availability of small arms to abusive actors. According to one study:

> The world is flooded with small arms and light weapons numbering at least 500 million, enough for one of every 12 people on earth. Legal authorities control most of these, but when they fall into the hands . . . of irregular forces, small arms bring devastation. They exacerbate conflict, spark refugee flows, undermine the rule of law, and spawn a culture of violence and impunity. In short, small arms are a threat to peace and development, to democracy and human rights.[2]

The ease by which weapons and ammunition were accessible to the various factions and the technical assistance provided by mercenaries with training and planning aggravated the risk of disorder and instability of the sub-region.

In Liberia, mercenaries were key players in the conflict, whether as fighters controlling some areas with precious minerals and other natural resources or as suppliers of arms. Although the different protagonists, especially the mercenaries, were engaged in other businesses, it is said that these were a cover for their mercenary activities.[3] The United Nations Inter-Agency Mission to West Africa was alarmed by the incapacity of the states in the region to control the movements of rebels and to "monitor and curb the illegal flow of arms and the formation of militia groups."[4] These groups are independent from state control and ensure their own security by contracting mercenaries. The easy exploitation of natural resources, such as timber and diamonds, also enables militias by forcibly enrolling local villagers (especially young boys) to finance their activities.

The United Nations reported that armed groups, militias and guerillas control at the very least one fifth of the diamonds marketed by collaborating either among themselves or with foreign countries and companies.[5] This form of business is attractive for actors whose primary objective is to make fast money and has proven to be possible in the absence of a functioning state because such activities require little capital investment.[6] Not only the rebels themselves or the nationals of neighboring states, but some Western countries and businessmen as well take advantage of the agony of the state to plunder its resources. Efforts to resolve these wars are generally unproductive because economic resources provide warlords with the means to enrich themselves and to continue financing their military campaigns.[7] Not surprisingly, battles are fought for the control of areas rich in economic resources, and many sources emphasize how all parties to the conflicts pursued a form of 'commercial insurgency.'[8] The dissemination of armed groups all over the sub-region is due to international and domestic factors. The end of superpower rivalry and the subsequent loss of geo-strategic interest in Sub-Saharan Africa restricted opportunities for foreign patronage. Many leaders could not continue to rely on an outside power to provide financial and military support to their regimes. These external factors, however, only partly explain the crisis of the post-colonial state. The crisis of legitimacy and the inability of the state to provide for its own security contributed to the proliferation of armed groups as state capacity control was in decline. The states cannot control the various armed groups in their territories, because they do not possess the military and material capacity to do so. They do not have the human resources either, because soldiers lack discipline, commitment, patriotism or the inclination to defend the state.[9] Soldiers are not only unmotivated, but they are also often corrupt and subversive.

Since the states cannot establish nor maintain order, the privatization of security is perceived as an insurance policy for unpopular, corrupt and collapsing regimes. State institutions are not obeyed because of the lack of authority and legitimacy. Citizens do not obey the rulers because they do not receive the reciprocal benefits for doing this. Since state's legitimacy is in decline and rulers no longer command sufficient resources for coercion, authority is threatened. Not the state, but security firms have the monopoly of violence, and political leaders seem unaware of the fact that these mercenaries are the biggest threat to the security of the state, to its independence, to its sovereignty, because at any time, they might decide to turn against those they are supposed to protect and rally to the militia groups. In these conflicts, all protagonists have a strong interest in seeing the conflict prolonged and they maintain insecurity and instability in several countries. They often have the means to do so because as an observer notes, "vast quantities of weapons, especially small arms, used to fight wars of independence, civil wars, and insurgencies remain in circulation and help fuel present conflicts."[10] These arms require little maintenance and can last for decades. They are available in important quantities, easy to transport, to buy and to use. For all these reasons, the Inter-Agency Mission to West Africa concluded that "conflicts can no longer be viewed in isolation, nor humanitarian intervention, peace and security problems be viewed as specific and internal."[11]

In fact, the Liberian conflict gained a greater diffusion and a sub-regional dimension partly due to the *modus operandi* of armed groups that have already crossed borders and have established and developed regional connections, techniques and organizations. Their mobility, alliances and counter-alliances, fusions and scissions, the fluidity of borders, huge stockpiles of weapons circulating from one conflict to another, complicate the situation and call for a revision of what is called internal conflict. Rebel and bandit groups wrestled vast tracts of territory away from central political control. Liberia was a warlord state where central authority evaporated and various groups exercised a network of alliances to contain and control strategic resources in the region outside government control. As a recent UN report observed:

> Despite the devastation that armed conflicts bring, there are many who profit from chaos and lack of accountability, and who have little or no interest in stopping a conflict and much interest to prolonging it. Very high on the list of those who profit from conflict in Africa are international arms merchants. Also high on the list, usually, are the protagonists themselves. In Liberia, the control and exploitation of diamonds, timber and other raw materials was one of the principal objectives of the warring factions.[12]

ECOWAS leaders and the UN, through the Program for Coordination and Assistance for Security and Development, have tried to address the problem of the alarming proliferation of small arms and light weapons and its negative impact on long-term sustainable development. The program suggested to the heads of states of ECOWAS to sign in Abuja on October 1998 a Moratorium on the Importation, Exportation and Manufacture of Light Weapons. They also approved a 'Code of Conduct' in Lomé, Togo, in December 1999, spelling out the concrete actions to be taken by member states to implement the Moratorium with the long-term aim of tackling widespread instability and insecurity in the West African sub-region.[13] But despite these actions, the results were disappointing to the Inter-Agency Mission to West Africa because of the lack of political commitment or of tangible signs of implementation. Moreover, sanctions against countries contravening such arrangements were not enforced and the ceremonies of arms reduction were symbolic, with "highly publicized efforts," but without tangible effects.[14]

To make matters worse, refugees became part of the security problem. It is estimated that by the time African leaders met in Banjul the 6th and 7th of August 1990 to address the situation, nearly 500,000 Liberian refugees had flooded into Guinea, Côte d'Ivoire and Sierra Leone. Armed groups held nationals from Nigeria, Ghana and Sierra Leone hostage. Most of these countries lack sufficient infrastructure to absorb the influx and migration of people. These movements of people became an additional source of insecurity for the citizens of the host states because various rebels infiltrated refugee camps to launch assaults. Situated near borders, these camps facilitate such activities and they were also repeatedly attacked by local populations. These events, as well their profound repercussions, set up the discussion of the justifications advanced for ECOWAS actions under regional security.

THE LEGAL FRAMEWORK

Any legal basis for action must justify itself in a specific context, taking into account actual contingencies. As explained in the preceding chapter, when ECOWAS intervened in Liberia, the main justification used was humanitarian, and it is captured in the following statement:

> . . . The wanton destruction of human life and property and the displacement of persons . . . the massive damage in various forms being caused by the armed conflict to the stability and survival of the entire Liberian nation; and concern . . . about the plight of foreign nationals, particularly the citizens of the community who are seriously affected by the conflict; and considering that law and order in Liberia had broken down . . . to find a peaceful and lasting solution to the conflict and to put an end to the situation which is seriously disrupting the normal life of innocent citizens in Liberia.[15]

ECOWAS did not base its first decision to intervene on regional security grounds because the conflict became a regional crisis only after the deployment of ECOMOG. According to Babangida:

> [In] a sub-region of 16 countries where one out of three West Africans is a Nigerian, it is imperative that any regime in this country should relentlessly strive towards the prevention or avoidance of the deterioration of any crisis which threatens to jeopardize or compromise the stability, prosperity and security of the sub-region. . . . We believe that if [a crisis is] of such level that has the potentials to threaten the stability, peace and security of the sub-region, Nigeria in collaboration with others in this sub-region, is duty-bound to react or respond in appropriate manner necessary to. . . . ensure peace, tranquility and harmony.[16]

According to the above-quoted text, regional insecurity was not established at the beginning of the war despite the fact that Taylor invaded the country from neighboring Côte d'Ivoire. In fact, regional insecurity was to a degree an unanticipated consequence of the intervention. It was when several states became involved in the crisis in varying degrees that the conflict escalated both in terms of the level of violence and in terms of its expansion to other countries, Sierra Leone, Guinea, essentially. As a result, instability, large movements of people, the proliferation of arms, the increasing number of combatants that included children, exacerbated a spiral of violence and a reign of terror in civilians. Due to the permeability of boundaries, rebel groups established bases across borders in order to gain access to resources or to create sanctuaries from state security forces. Therefore, when government forces engaged rebels in combats, the effects of the war spread across borders and into neighboring states, hence the regional dimension of the conflict. What do general norms of international law say about this situation?

Some questions that do not address the core of the debate have been raised. It has been argued that because ECOWAS did not define clearly what was meant by 'regional security,' it was difficult to justify intervention on that ground. It has also been noted that the lack of consensus before the intervention as well as the prohibition of interference in internal matters of member states contained in the 1981 Protocol made the intervention illegal.[17] Other ambiguities were encountered, notably the applicability of the Protocol in situations like that of Liberia, because the Protocol makes no distinction between internal and external threats and fails to specify what types of conflicts within one member state constitute a threat to the region.[18]

On procedural grounds, one author notes that President Doe's request for intervention was sent not to the Chairman of the Authority, but to the Chair of the Council of Ministers.[19] He further notes that at the time the letter was written, Doe "was not in control of the country, having been confined to the Executive Mansion for months" and that the decision to dispatch intervention forces should have been taken by the full summit of ECOWAS rather than by a subcommittee like the Standing Mediation Committee. Furthermore, the author asserts that ECOMOG intervention included peace enforcement measures and therefore went beyond both the spirit and the letter of the action sought by Doe, who initially only requested a peacekeeping force.[20]

Unfortunately, these arguments are legally weak because they do not correctly address the issues, and the questions they are raising are not the most important, especially if one looks at the general principles of international law. Moreover, their conclusions are erroneous because they fail to examine correctly the most relevant legal norm on that issue:

the right of collective self-defense, which is an inherent right, a principle of international and customary law, a principle as fundamental as the principle of non-intervention and non-use of force. But before going further, their conclusions on the applicability of ECOWAS mechanisms need to be corrected.

ECOWAS treaties reaffirm the general principle of non-use of force, and also prohibit acts of subversion, hostility or aggression against the political independence of member states.[21] In pursuance of this obligation, members are committed to prevent foreigners or other residents in their countries from committing such acts, and in particular from using their territory as a base for subversion.[22] The protocol on Non-Aggression was complemented by a Protocol on Mutual Defense in 1981, which declares in its preamble that states "firmly resolve to safeguard and consolidate the independence and the sovereignty of member states against foreign intervention." The treaty, a mixture of collective security and defense, completed the general structure of ECOWAS. Armed threat or aggression against a member state, it is reaffirmed, constitutes a threat or aggression against the entire community.[23]

Under the terms of the 1981 Protocol, member states have resolved to give mutual aid and assistance for defense against any armed threat or aggression,[24] and are required to set aside military units for an "Allied Armed Forces of the Community" (AAFC).[25] The AAFC are to be placed under a Forces Commander appointed by the Authority (on a recommendation of the Defense Council), to be used as a peacekeeping force between two member states engaged in an armed conflict, or to address an internal conflict in a member state that is actively maintained and sustained from outside ECOWAS when requested by the member state.[26] In such a situation, aid is to be provided when requested by a member state facing an external armed threat or aggression.[27] The ECOWAS forces are not to intervene if a conflict remains "purely internal."[28]

Contrary to what has been argued, if full effect is given to Article 4 (a) and 4 (b) of the ECOWAS Protocol relating to Mutual Defense, it allowed intervention in the Liberian crisis under regional collective security because Article 17 (1) of the same Protocol clearly states: "In a case where an internal conflict in a Member State of the Community is actively maintained and sustained from outside, the provisions of Articles 6, 9 and 16 of this Protocol shall apply." Article 17 and Article 4 have to be read together. Intervention in member states is only prohibited when the conflict is *purely* internal but not when " . . . internal armed conflict within any Member State engineered and supported actively from outside [is] likely to endanger the security and peace of the entire community."[29]

The Liberian war was an internally generated conflict, but was actively maintained and sustained by outside forces. Charles Taylor's insurrection was supported by Burkina Faso and Côte d'Ivoire, two members of the community, and by Libya, a state outside the region. Not all conflicts occurring within the territory of a state are purely internal and deemed to be excluded from the application of the Protocol. What is not rational, however, is that member states participate in the destabilization of their own region. Therefore, law is important in the examination of the conflict, so are other contingencies.

The origin of the assistance (internal or external), referred to as "outside support" in the Protocol, does not seem to be determinant in my view; and either origin can produce the same legal consequences not necessarily with regard to ECOWAS treaties but at least to general principles of international law. Support can count as an attack and justifies the right to self-defense, as will be examined later. Assuming that the pact's provisions on internal conflict, sustained and maintained from outside apply only in cases of extra regional support for internal strife, the intervention met the criterion for a collective response because of the involvement of Libya, an external member. This is a case of collective defense, in case of external intervention or support from outside. But because the mechanism also contains elements of collective security, the Protocol is not exclusively directed against the threat or the use of force from outside the community, but also from within. Article 15 can justify this interpretation, and the legitimate defense of the territories of the community justified intervention by AAFC.[30]

The dynamics of the conflict and the spillover into the regional level, give relevance to a recognized principle of international law, the doctrine of abatement, defined as a "legal justification for forceful intervention by an outside power, or by a regional organization, in what are otherwise considered the internal affairs of a neighboring country."[31] The doctrine fits the case. The action of the community was justifiable under the legal right of collective self-defense by an extreme situation of necessity especially when national or regional stability is threatened by warfare which, as envisaged by the definition of abatement spills into neighboring states in the form of hot pursuit or fleeing guerillas, or when guerillas take unauthorized refuge or establish military bases across a poorly defended or isolated frontier. This is exactly what happened in Liberia. Not only as a preventive but also as a remedial action, the community was right to combat subversion and disorder. It was an intervention to reestablish order, and this is legitimate.

As mentioned earlier, Article 16 of the protocol was perceived as a collective regime of security. When aggression is directed against a Member state, the head of state of that country must send a written request for assistance to the current Chairman of the Authority of ECOWAS. A commentator has noted that Doe's request was not sent to the Chairman of the Authority, but to the Chair of the Council of Ministers. The author is correct to note that the request was not properly directed according to ECOWAS dispositions. That initiative could have even reinforced Doe because it can be interpreted as a solicited intervention, which is entirely lawful. The extent to which this irregularity should matter remains uncertain, but this does not at all nullify the right of self-defense that the head of state has under international law depositions. A victim state can declare that it has been attacked or destabilized and request aid. There is no general rule in the UN Charter or specific procedure under customary law regulating that declaration. Doe, the head of State, not necessarily referring to that point of international law, did send, however, a letter to his fellows to declare his country was being attacked:

> Right now in the suburbs of Monrovia thousands have been displaced by the NPFL Forces, homes have been destroyed, hundreds slaughtered, even before their dubious victory is achieved. I am therefore concerned that the fighting could accelerate in Monrovia and thus inflame the suffering of the people of Liberia.[32]

President Doe went on to describe the entry of dissidents from Côte d'Ivoire as a continuing problem: "they use that country as a springboard to come and kill people in Liberia, then we feel that that government supports what those people are doing."[33] He then provided evidence that his country was attacked and that he was soliciting intervention.

It has been noted against that argument that Doe was not in control of the country when he was sending the request and was besieged at the Executive Mansion. But this did not prevent him from requesting assistance. After all he was *de jure* the internationally recognized president of Liberia and no other government was recognized except his. Although contested by factions, he still had prerogatives as a head of state. Nor is it convincing to argue that the Protocol was dormant for a long time and had never been implemented because no mechanism was in place.[34] That the ECOWAS states do not have standing troops for the Community does not remove their obligations under the Protocol to take appropriate measures if it is found that an internal armed conflict within a member state is engineered or actively supported by external forces, especially if such support constitutes a threat to the security and peace of the community.

Opponents of the intervention on the basis of ECOWAS' constitutional structure lamented the fact that it was the SMC that took the decision to intervene and not the Authority of Heads of State and government.[35] This surprising argument is not tenable. According to ECOWAS treaty of May

28, 1975, the institutions of the Community are the Authority of Heads of State and Government, the Council of Ministers and the Executive Secretariat.[36] The authority is the principal governing institution of the community,[37] and its decisions are binding "on all institutions of the Community."[38] Under these provisions, the ratification by the ECOWAS heads of states of the Standing Mediation Committee's initial decision to intervene, coupled with article 4 (b) of the defense pact, is sufficient to validate that decision for purposes of the community.[39] The treaty provides for technical and other specialized commissions and the Authority is empowered from time to time to establish other commissions, as is necessary.[40] On the basis of these articles, the creation of the SMC was legal.

Finally, the weakest point of the examination of the legality of the operation is that none of the authors has examined the legality of the ECOWAS intervention with reference to the position of the International Court of Justice. Most of the doubts and questions raised by the authors on the applicability of the ECOWAS treaty are not as problematic because they are resolved under general principles of international law, especially under the inherent right of self-defense. As already discussed, the general prohibition of the use of force allows for very few exceptions. One of those is the right of self-defense, and more particularly, given the general disorder in the region, the right to collective self-defense. With regard to that right, article 51 of the UN Charter refers to the "inherent right" or *droit naturel,* which all states possess in the event of armed attack. It covers both collective and individual self-defense. In law, these enjoy the same recognition as the important principle of prohibition of use of force. Both principles are also contained in the "Declaration on the Principles of International Law Concerning friendly relations and Cooperation among States in accordance with the Charter of the United Nations." After affirming the prohibition of the use of force, this declaration continues: "Nothing in the foregoing paragraphs shall be construed as enlarging or diminishing in any way the scope of the provisions of the Charter concerning cases in which the use of force is lawful." The General Assembly considers the right of individual and collective self-defense as a principle of customary international law. Put differently, the non-use of force and self-defense are two faces of the same coin.

On the conditions governing its use, the Charter is silent. However, since the decision of the International Court of Justice in the *Nicaragua Case,* there has been agreement on the specific conditions on the nature of the acts, which can be treated as constituting armed attacks. The Court spelled out the following set of conditions relevant in the Liberian case. It considered that "an armed attack must be understood as including not merely action by regular armed forces across an international border . . ."

but also "the sending by and on behalf of a State of armed bands, groups, irregulars or mercenaries, which carry out acts of armed force against another State." [41] In other words, the sending of armed bands to the territory of another state is an act of aggression. Although in the Nicaragua case, the Court did not state a level of magnitude, one can assume that the conflict in Liberia could be qualified as such, thus justifying the action.

Extending training, financial patronage, encouragement or support of incursion, in whatever form, in a member state or any state is against the rules, norms and principles of international law and can justify the right of self-defense because it represents an attack. It is in contradiction to the right to territorial integrity and political independence. The International Court of Justice has made it clear that the notion of armed attack includes not only acts by armed bands, rebels and guerillas but also *assistance* to rebels by the provision of weapons or logistical or other support.[42] Such assistance amounts to intervention in internal affairs, and is regarded as illegal. In its examination of the right of self-defense against armed attacks, individual or collective, the Court recognized that the General Assembly's "Definition of aggression" "may be taken to reflect customary international law."[43] That definition, accepted as customary international law, is particularly relevant in the Liberian case and stipulates in part, in article 3, that:

Any of the following acts, regardless of a declaration of war, shall . . . qualify as an act of aggression:

(a) The invasion or attack by armed forces of a State of the territory of another State, or any occupation, however temporary, resulting from such invasion or attack, or any annexation by the use of force of the territory of another State or part thereof;

(b) Bombardment of the armed forces of a State against the territory of another State or the use of any weapons by a State against the territory of another State;

(c) The blockade of the ports or coasts of a State by the armed forces of another State;

(d) An armed attack by the forces of another State on the land, sea or air forces, or marine and air fleets of another State;

(e) The use of armed forces of one State which are within the territory of another State with the agreement of the receiving State, in contravention of the conditions provided for in the agreement or any extension of their presence in such territory beyond the termination of the agreement;

(f) The action of a State in allowing its territory, which it has placed at the disposal of another State, to be used by that other State for perpetrating an act of aggression against a third State;

(g) The sending by or on behalf of State of armed bands, groups, irregulars or mercenaries, which carry out acts of armed force against another State of such gravity as to amount to the acts listed above, or its substantial involvement therein.

Support of militias and other groups against their own government or any other is unlawful and is in opposition to the ethics of diplomatic relations. In Liberia, there was direct and deliberate external support that was consequential for the conflict.

For a fuller appreciation of the difficulties raised by the legality of the intervention, it is worthy to note that aside from Libya, the conflict was maintained by some ECOWAS' states reconfirming that controversies and incoherence should be kept in mind when analyzing the legal framework. Leaders based their decisions on the need to protect regional security; while it appears that those same states were responsible for the disorder. Therefore, Liberia does not constitute a good example for moving beyond the principle of non-intervention. On the contrary, states should refrain from manipulating the internal affairs of other states. Respecting the principle of non-intervention is indeed a moral value. Contrary to what has been written Liberia demonstrates not the obsolescence, but the relevance of the non-intervention norm, because it is the involvement of ECOWAS states that contributed largely to endanger regional peace and security, raising the issue of the essential role of the Security Council in such situations.

Chapter Four
Lip Service Foreign Policy

During the Liberian war ECOWAS leaders orchestrated a series of diplomatic initiatives, which sought to establish the basis for peace in Liberia. These initiatives repeatedly failed because of a serious lack of commitment by the factions involved and because ECOWAS leaders themselves were not neutral. Surprisingly, despite these difficulties the leaders of ECOWAS decided to move forward and endorsed a new legal framework drafted by the Ministers of Foreign Affairs, Defense and Internal Affairs for a security mechanism designed to provide ECOWAS with the capacity to standardize its operations in managing conflict in West Africa. The new mechanism, adopted at Lomé in December 1999, represents a new legal and political blueprint to conflict management in the sub-region and has been justified as an attempt to consolidate the lessons learned from the ECOMOG intervention. This chapter will provide a narrative of these negotiations and the problems raised by their implementation. It will then analyze the new mechanism adopted and some of the difficulties it contains.

CONFUSED DIPLOMACY AND CREDIBILITY DEFICIT

There were fourteen peace agreements with nine accords between 1990 and 1994, and it is impossible to focus on each of them. They will be studied in three sections. The first considers the accords signed before the July 1993 Cotonou Accord; the second looks at the Cotonou accord itself, while the third analyses the post-Cotonou agreements. The Cotonou accord was the most comprehensive because of the supporting diplomatic efforts by the United Nations and the Organization of African Unity.

BEFORE COTONOU

Seven major ECOWAS-sponsored agreements were signed before the Cotonou Accord but none of them was implemented.[1] The Bamako, Banjul and Lomé Agreements may be considered as the first stage of ECOWAS diplomacy. Charles Taylor, the main warlord, accepted to come to the negotiation table after he was displaced from Monrovia by ECOMOG troops.[2] At the Bamako meeting, Taylor's NPFL, along with the Armed Forces of Liberia (AFL) and the Independent National Patriotic Front of Liberia (INPFL), the two factions active at the time, committed themselves to the ECOWAS Peace Plan and to an immediate ceasefire agreement.[3] In Banjul, they pledged to organize a national conference which would reconstitute the Interim Government of National Unity (IGNU). In February 1991 at Lomé, modalities of the ceasefire were specified. ECOMOG was given the prime role in disarming the three factions. ECOMOG was also to supervise the handing in of weapons and the registration of troops.[4]

Only Charles Taylor of the NPFL signed these agreements under intense military and diplomatic pressure. In securing Monrovia, ECOMOG was accused of collaborating with AFL and INPFL forces to resist the NPFL advance.[5] In this context of mutual suspicion, hopes for disarmament were slim. The accords were contested by the NPFL who refused to recognize the authority of the conference, and set up a strategy of consolidating its National Patriotic Reconstruction Assembly Government (NPRAG). Thus, the interim government was reconstituted without NPFL participation.

The pre-Cotonou diplomatic process was revitalized in June 1991 with the signing of the Yamoussoukro I accord. It well augured a rapprochement between the NPFL and IGNU and built the impetus for the three further accords. Under the leadership of the late President Houphouët-Boigny of Côte d'Ivoire, the Yamoussoukro peace initiatives involved a "Committee of five,"[6] as well as Charles Taylor and Amos Sawyer, President of the IGNU.[7] The accord was also supported by Jimmy Carter's International Negotiation Network in monitoring the ceasefire. The involvement of the INN was meant to enhance the acceptability of ECOMOG among the various Liberian factions, given the suspicion caused by its previous actions.

Diplomacy, however, did not show any sign of progress and between July and October 1991 two further accords (Yamoussoukro II and III) were signed but were immediately broken when one group decided that the accord was to its disadvantage. African facilitators were accused of unfairness. Babangida had strong animosity against Taylor. Houphouët-Boigny, who replaced him, was later accused of partiality because his desire was to install Charles Taylor.[8] The lack of progress was mainly due to a lack of trust among the different actors involved and to divisions among ECOWAS members. Some procedures were also incoherent, as for example, the decisions to invite as observers Guinea and Sierra Leone, two member states concerned with the spill-over of the conflict. The two countries refused to participate in the meetings.[9] The Yamoussoukro II meeting extended the consultations to the various parties to the conflict, but this second meeting turned out to be somewhat unrealistic because only one Liberian warlord (Taylor) was present at the meeting; thus this agreement had no value.[10]

The great effort continued and in October 1991 a Yamoussoukro IV agreement was signed. This accord gave a central role to ECOMOG and welcomed the deployment of Sénégalese troops. Among the items discussed was the formation of an *ad hoc* Supreme Court for the adjudication of disputes arising from future elections. The destabilizing role of the Liberian rebels in Sierra Leone was also discussed, and it was agreed that all hostile foreign forces should be withdrawn from the territory of Sierra Leone. The meeting concluded that a buffer zone to be monitored by ECOMOG should be created between the two countries.[11] While this accord reflected a better appreciation of the conflict, it was nevertheless over-optimistic because ECOMOG could not cover the whole of Liberia and monitor all entry points into the country.[12] The accord was also exaggeratedly unrealistic in its timing because it envisaged that the encampment, disarmament, demobilization, and the necessary conditions for peace designed to build confidence among the parties and a proper atmosphere for elections could be implemented in sixty days.[13]

It was not surprising, therefore, that the Yamoussoukro IV accord was jeopardized like its predecessors, by a lack of factional commitment and by antagonism among ECOWAS members. Neither the AFL nor the INPFL, nor the new United Liberation Movement of Liberia for Democracy (ULIMO), which had come into existence a few months earlier, was present at the relevant meetings. Not only was the accord technically flawed, but once again, suspicions undermined its implementation. Nigeria feared "francophone" collaboration with the NPFL, because Taylor was supported by Burkina Faso, and had invaded Liberia from Côte d'Ivoire whose president was leading the negotiations. According to one author, fear led elements within ECOMOG to provide covert support to the emerging United Liberation Movement of Liberia for Democracy, which was supposed to oppose the NPFL-backed insurrection in Sierra Leone.[14] These ECOMOG enforcement actions invented by Nigeria brought out tensions regarding Nigeria's military approaches to the conflict. As Eboe Hutchful puts it:

The Ghanaians were constantly perplexed by the *modus operandi* of
the Nigerians, who they found "very, very unconventional" in the
administration of their forces. Ghanaian officers were critical in private
of what they perceived as the patronage relationship between Nigerian
officers and soldiers, the involvement of Nigerian soldiers in various
corrupt and illicit businesses, and command practices that compro-
mised discipline and operational security. [15]

In sum, the Yamoussoukro initiatives did not automatically entail support
for the role of EGOMOG, or even any serious commitment to the implementation of all Yamoussoukro's provisions. The negotiations exposed
Houphouët's inability to control his NPFL client and confirmed the percep-
tion that the francophone states were in fact the backers of the NPFL.

COTONOU

The Cotonou Accord was the most comprehensive agreement signed on
Liberia. Since ECOWAS members were not neutral, external parties were
needed. The lack of neutrality when regional actors are involved is the
Achilles' heel of the idea of delegating peace operations to regional bodies. The accord was facilitated by the collaboration of the UN and the
OAU. Under the auspices of the OAU, Tanzania and Uganda sent contingents to expand ECOMOG and increase its acceptability in the eyes of
the various armed groups involved. The Cotonou accord stipulated that
the belligerents should observe a new ceasefire to be monitored by ECO-
MOG and a United Nations Observer Mission in Liberia (UNOMIL),
whose observers should enjoy complete freedom of movement throughout the country.[16] The parties agreed not to import weapons or use the
ceasefire for a military build-up (as had happened so often before), nor
to engage in other activities that would violate the ceasefire, and they
should recognize that the ECOWAS-UN arms embargo would remain in
force.[17]

Under the partnership of ECOMOG and UNOMIL, the problem of
impartiality was resolved, and the parties expressed their willingness and
finally their agreement to abide by a disarmament and demobilization program. All weapons and warlike materials were to be handed over to ECO-
MOG and monitored by UN observers. Combatants of the various factions
as well as non-combatants carrying arms should report and hand over their
weapons to ECOMOG, which would be allowed to disarm any (ex-) com-
batant or non-combatant in case of non-compliance, as well as to search
for and recover hidden weapons. However, in all cases UNOMIL would

have to observe ECOMOG activities.[18] The supervision of ECOMOG by UNOMIL is evidence of the lack of trust that ECOMOG generated during its own campaign.

Cotonou also established some political measures. The civilian Interim Government of National Unity would be replaced by the Liberian National Transitional Government (LNTG), which would provide essential government services during a transitional period.[19] The executive branch of the LNTG would consist of a five-member 'Council of State,' made up of representatives of the NPFL, ULIMO and IGNU, with two remaining members selected from nine candidates, nominated by the signatory parties on the basis of a detailed selection procedure.[20] On the legislature, the parties agreed that the Transitional Legislative Assembly (TLA) should be a unicameral body composed of thirty-five members. Both IGNU and NPFL would each be entitled to thirteen members and ULIIMO to nine members, with the right to nominate the speaker from one of its members in the Assembly.[21]

To guarantee continuity, the existing structure of the Supreme Court remained unchanged. It was agreed that ULIMO should have the right to nominate the fifth member of the Court according to established criteria to fill the vacancy that currently existed.[22] Significantly, anyone holding positions in the LNTG, whether in the Council of State, the TLA, the Elections Commission or the Supreme Court, would be ineligible to stand for the projected legislative and presidential elections.[23] The Cotonou agreement marked a major turning point in ECOWAS diplomacy for a number of reasons. Firstly, it represented the end of the era in which factions signed merely as half-hearted or duplicitous responses to external pressure. With the Cotonou Accord, the peace process began to focus more specifically on the relationships and interests of the factions themselves, and hence acquired a much more Liberian character. Secondly, it opened at the same time a new stage in the peace process, during which Liberian politics came to be dominated by armed factions. One observer was alarmed by the fact that ECOMOG's efforts to establish a power-sharing agreement between the various factions went so far as to risk the elimination of the civilian state.[24] Predictably, Liberia's civil society reacted unenthusiastically to Cotonou as well as to later accords. The agreements were seen as "political rewards" for armed violence, a "power-for-gun policy."[25]

Given these factors, the process of the implementation of the accords also ran into practical difficulties. UNOMIL was too small to constitute a force, demonstrating clearly the UN's *service minimum* reaction. Furthermore, the delays of getting additional troops and contingents from other African states led to new inertia. Finally, while extremely detailed, Cotonou nevertheless suffered from various acts of omissions, because it contained no provision for resolving the disputes that all too often arose from appointments to the executive of a transitional government. The immediate consequence of these omissions was to plague the functioning and the efficacy of the administration for months after its installation.[26] This problem could have been taken into consideration, since it was well known that the factions were fighting over access to state resources and control of state institutions.

At the leadership level, an elite hungry for personal power was one of the salient features of the Liberian war, and this elite expressed itself after the signature of the Cotonou Accord. Because the agreement failed to clarify the exact role of the Council of State, once appointed, not only did several of the representatives of the factions break ties with the factions that had sponsored them, but, as decision-makers, they were never serving the needs of all Liberians. This is also evidence of Liberia's weak political and institutional experience regarding the role of the administration. The immediate consequence of the failure of the Council of State members to represent even their factional interests upon assuming office was a sustained instability, fueled by the leaders of the warring factions because of their strong interests, particularly economic ones.[27] Finally, considering the magnitude of divergences, the accord placed unrealistic expectations on a deeply divided LNTG, which in turn was paralyzed and did not control any more territory than IGNU had done, while ECOMOG's expansion across Liberia was halted. By the 1994, the Cotonou Accord became inoperative.

THE POST-COTONOU ACCORDS

Between the collapse of the Cotonou Accord and the outbreak of renewed fighting in April 1996, three new agreements were signed: the Akosombo Accord in September 1994, the Accra Clarification of December 1994, and the August 1995 Abuja Accord. The principal objective of the Akosombo Accord was to grant the LNTG and the dominant factions a more central role in the management of Liberian affairs. To this end, it amended the Cotonou Accord in a number of ways. First, it placed the responsibility of overseeing the peace agreement not only on ECOMOG and UNOMIL, but also on the security forces of the LNTG.[28] Second, it ceded effective control of the Council of State to the more powerful factions, removing the requirement of consensus-based decision-making and instituting the authority of a simple majority.[29] Third, it permitted the factions to review the status of their appointees at all levels of the administration at any time.[30]

The main issues addressed in the Akosombo Accord centered on the problems of appointments and nominations. Strong resistance was registered by ECOWAS members, notably Nigerians, and by a range of Liberian political parties and civilian interest groups. A major concern was that the agreement seemed to favor disproportionately the NPFL. Many Liberian citizens were outraged and generally interpreted Akosombo as an attempt to install a military junta.[31] Compared with the three signatories to the Akosombo Accord, no fewer than eight groups signed the Accra Clarification that brought new groups into the peace process, along with those who had searched for a solution. After signing the Accra Clarification on 21 December 1994, however, the parties failed to reach an agreement on the composition and chairmanship of the Council of State.

The 1995 and 1996 Abuja Accords were the last to be concluded in this tour of African capitals characterized by disorderly diplomacy. The main objective of the Abuja 1995 Accord was to bring the leaders of all warring factions into the transitional government, which was installed in September 1995.[32] As such, it represented the fulfillment of the aspirations of the post-Cotonou peace process.[33] It did not, however, bring peace to Liberia and the factions continued to guard their territorial and commercial resources jealously, with ongoing violence among various sub-groups and individuals who sought to consolidate and extend their power within the framework of the LNTG. An increasing number of factional fighters entered Monrovia to ensure the security of their leaders. Perhaps the most important achievement of the Abuja Accord was that it managed to bring the leaders of the warring factions into the transitional government.

In a second meeting, also held in Abuja and which produced the Abuja II Accord in August 1996, there was general recognition that it was time to end the conflict. This was the most important accord because it represented the peace pact, and that which history will record as having officially ended the conflict. The first problem that Abuja II resolved was the problem of the Council of State. The first important decision taken was the removal, as the head of the Council of the State, of Wilton Sankawulo who himself admitted he had failed.[34] Mrs. Ruth Perry was appointed as the new chairwoman. The second achievement of Abuja II was the drawing up of a timetable for the ceasefire, the demobilization and the conduct of elections. The revised arrangement was the following:

- Disarmament, demobilization and repatriation: November 22 1996 to January 31,1997;

- Resignation of the members of the Council of State and other holders of public office who wish to run for election,

- Preparation for elections from January 20 1997 to April 15 1997;

- Presidential elections: May 30 1997.

This accord appeared to be an emergency exit. Disarmament is a necessary precondition for law, order and peace but it is not itself sufficient to achieve these goals. It was never achieved and after the signature of the accord the situation remained insecure and explosive in Liberia for many years. The leaders of the factions failed to comply with the Abuja II Accord and the warlords' promise to complete the disarmament of their fighters by December 31, 1996 was never honored.

Regarding the organization of elections, it is to be noted that the peace initiatives were not designed to build a nation, but to appease the warlords. Efforts were not made to build trust, reconciliation, civil society and human capital. Once again, an important actor is needed here: the state, a responsive institution that can pave the way for participatory democracy, and reduce anxiety and uncertainty in the aftermath of a traumatizing war. With the war ending in February 1997 and the elections being held on July 19th of the same year, both reconciliation and rebuilding a troubled society were needed. As Lowenkopf noted: "Apart from a general skepticism about the promise and legitimizing qualities of most elections in Africa, even if unchallengably free and fair . . . the case for early elections in Liberia that would establish a government of and for the people is feeble and technically unmanageable."[35]

The ability of holding elections was very new to most Liberian officials, and the process needed further elaboration if the intended goal was truly to help build a better future in Liberia. Sadly, the elections were a ritualistic hypocrisy intended to put a warlord in power, in this case Charles Taylor. After the elections on 19 July 1997, the results were announced on 24 July, with Charles Taylor winning 75.3 percent of the presidential vote, making a run-off unnecessary. The only reason why Liberians voted for Charles Taylor was their desire for peace. They saw Taylor's victory, not Taylor himself, as the inescapable condition of peace and stability. Liberians feared a return to war if Taylor lost the elections. Thus, the issue of peace dominated the elections. According to Terrence Lyons, a senior adviser for the Carter Center in Liberia, many Liberians believed that if Taylor lost the election, the country would return to war.[36] They feared that Charles Taylor would be another Savimbi and one quoted voter admitted: "He killed my father but I'll vote for him. He started all this and he's going to fix it."[37] Liberia was a political jungle, and with Taylor's election, warlords and firepower became the guarantors of democracy that they will never bring to Liberia. Liberians reasoned that voting for Taylor was the price to pay to move away from war. They therefore abandoned the most important political good that is democracy. The Liberian elections were cynical where democracy was a deferred dream. After the elections, as one may assume, Taylor failed to meet the expectations of keeping the peace, let alone rebuilding the country's economy, logistic and social infrastructure, or of integrating the population into the political sphere. It is fallacious to pretend that elections supervised by the international community bring about political pluralism. It was not certainly Taylor's objectives.

Many countries are organizing elections. Elections are flourishing but democracy is not. Fareed Zakaria reminds us that elections do not necessarily bring protection of individual liberties and adherence to the rule of law.[38] Many of the new regimes are "electoral democracies" "but not liberal democracies." Samuel P. Huntington had noted that what he termed "the Third Wave" was not necessarily conducive to democracy: "[e]lections, open, free and fair, are the essence of democracy, the inescapable sine qua non condition . . . Governments produced by elections may be inefficient, corrupt, shortsighted, irresponsible, dominated by special interests, and incapable of adopting policies demanded by the public good."[39] At best, all that the international community can do in this matter is to support a national government; it cannot replace the state nor can it export democracy. If the challenge is to build peace and to work in order to restore the rule of law, it remains to be seen how transition from war to peace and then to democratization is possible without a pact of reciprocity between citizens and a functioning state. The challenge, therefore is to restore the state and insist on its relevance rather than saying it is obsolete and pretending that observers can re-establish it.

One of the main weaknesses of the negotiations and of the several accords lay in seeking always to accommodate the demands of armed groups rather than building civic and political institutions. But is it really possible to do it from outside? The answer is no. That pact can only come from within. The accords were vulnerable to the emergence of new factions and their *desiderata*. After the elections and when the international community declared victory and went home, Liberia was in a profound situation of chaos. The country remains anarchic due to the failure by the international community to enforce the embargoes on illicit trade, which was prolonging the war, human rights violations, civilian distress and regional insecurity six years after the official end of the conflict. Incoherence explains the nebulous mediation of ECOWAS. If its objectives were to protect a civilian state, then the deployment of ECOMOG and the resolute defense of the IGNU are understandable. Less so are the attempts to pressure the rebels into a peace process they never wanted. On the other hand, if the idea was to minimize instability by seeking a neutral compromise, then the partisan collaboration of ECOMOG as well as the support extended to armed groups by member states makes little sense. In short, ECOWAS itself was driven by uncertainty and by competing interests. The subsequent decision to move forward and to institutionalize into a form of a treaty the experience of ECOMOG's involvement in Liberia and Sierra Leone also represents a very controversial decision as will now be examined.

ECOWAS' NEW SECURITY MECHANISM: LEGAL AND POLITICAL CONTROVERSIES

Following the interventions in Liberia and Sierra Leone, the member states of ECOWAS adopted a new Protocol Relating to the Mechanism for Conflict Prevention, Management, and Security at Lomé, Togo, on December 10, 1999. The treaty is the organization's constitution on regional security.

IDIOSYNCRACIES AND CONJECTURES

The major development of ECOWAS after the Liberian war was to introduce changes in the previous pattern of ECOWAS' instruments by legalizing intervention for humanitarian reasons or to prevent the overthrow of an elected government. The treaty is also intended to develop the capacity of ECOWAS to mount a military force. The first initiative came with the revision of the ECOWAS treaty and protocols in 1993, which made provisions for maintaining peace and security. Since then, member states have agreed, in principle, to set up formal mechanisms that would allow ECO-MOG to function as a security apparatus for the sub-region. Later, in October 1998, the West African Ministers of Foreign Affairs, Defense and Internal Affairs, drafted the framework for an ECOWAS security mechanism with the objective of standardizing its operations in managing conflicts in West Africa. The Security Mechanism, which was formally adopted at the ECOWAS summit at Lomé in December 1999, institutionalized a new approach to conflict management in West Africa by consolidating the experiences from the ECOMOG interventions. One of the most important and controversial clauses was the codification of the right to humanitarian intervention, which, intentionally or not, represented a move away from the traditional principle of non-intervention in internal affairs.

Without resolving the reservations raised by some member states on the use of force in domestic affairs that has been raised before the intervention in Liberia, as well as the continuous suspicions between the ECOWAS' leaders during and after its involvement in Liberia, the new mechanism empowers ECOWAS to intervene in internal conflicts of member states. Armed intervention can be undertaken not only in response to massive violations of human rights, but also in case of a breakdown of the rule of law.[40] If full effect is given to Article 25 of the new Mechanism, not only does the treaty institutionalize the practices of ECOWAS in Liberia and in Sierra Leone, but it also provides a controversial legal framework that removes the legal obligation of securing the Security Council's authorization for future intervention. To the extent that it incorporates the doctrine of humanitarian intervention and provides extensively for an early warning system, the Mechanism is probably the most ambitious legal attempt to regulate the problem of humanitarian intervention, not only by ECOWAS but also by any regional organization for that matter.[41] But as we shall see, this codification, together with the deep divisions among ECOWAS leaders, represent a risk for the sub-region.

The proactive engagement of ECOWAS leaders is difficult to justify. In legal terms, the new option taken is in contradiction with the obligation of peaceful settlement of disputes. One of the drawbacks of moving away from the traditional definition of peacekeeping is, as was the case in Liberia, not to leave a chance for negotiations and diplomacy to work. The traditional notion of peacekeeping refers to soldiers, organized or authorized by the UN and accepted by the parties to prevent interstate war and to reduce further hostilities between or among belligerent groups within a country.[42] The basic job of such forces is to keep the peace, to prevent people from killing others. Over the past few years, however, the international community decided, without any convincing justification, that this practice is obsolete. But traditional peacekeeping forces still have the advantage of being neutral and capable, through their presence, of separating warring parties, of calming heated passions, and of preventing renewed combat. During that time diplomacy can be given a chance. Ultimately, peacekeeping also has the advantage of conforming to international law because peacekeepers need the consent of the warring parties, and they do not use force except in the case of self-defense. The new mechanism, whose draft provisions were a virtual replication of the Protocol on Mutual Assistance and Defense,[43] totally jettisoned its classical peacekeeping dimension in favor of military intervention.[44] Thus the mechanism will apply to securing peace not only by traditional peacekeeping exercises, but also by using force, directly and unilaterally, as was done during the ECOWAS intervention in Sierra Leone.

The adoption by ECOWAS members of the term "collective security" in the new Mechanism is a clear evidence of the move in a direction that favors use of force rather than a peaceful conflict resolution method. But it is erroneously used. In its original meaning, collective security is understood as the utilization of the coercive capacity of the international community to combat illegal uses of armed force in situations that threaten international peace. But the West African organization meant only that member states' interventions in sub-regional conflicts will no longer be confined to peace-keeping, the main purpose for which ECOMOG was established in 1990.[45] The correct term is regional security. But more importantly this position is not coherent because it is some of the ECOWAS states that bore major responsibility for the fighting and disturbances in the sub-region by sup-porting militia groups. Non-intervention in the internal political dynamics of a sovereign country is obviously better than state sponsored violence aimed at destabilizing another country. Properly understood, non-intervention is not obsolete, it is an ethical principle.

In the domain of security, two scenarios justifying military interven-tion (an internal armed conflict within a member state actively supported from the outside and a conflict between two or more member states) have been covered earlier in this study.[46] The new Mechanism introduces an unprecedented innovation that empowers ECOMOG to undertake "human-itarian intervention *in support of* humanitarian disaster."[47] The article is poorly written, and it is reasonable to read the italicized words "in support of" to mean, "to prevent." This scenario is tricky for several reasons: it is a conscious and illegal effort to provide cover for future interventions by cod-ifying in a treaty the theory of humanitarian intervention, but it is also a risky and poor policy in light of the political divisions in the region. For these reasons it has no chance of concrete implementation, thereby under-mining the credibility of the leaders who signed it as the crisis in Côte d'Ivoire has revealed. Finally, it is a populist proclamation because the states lack the capacity.

We are here once again at the center of a paradox: the states that always opposed intervention as a violation of sovereignty are the first who enact it in the form of law. The new law represents a risk, as it can be instrumentalized and manipulated. The possibility of a *malo animo* inter-vention once again creates the need for the Security Council to authorize intervention before regional organizations can take the lead. Under the UN Charter, the Security Council's prior authorization is required when regional agencies or organizations act under Chapter VIII. But surprisingly, in the new Mechanism, Article 6 designates the Authority of ECOWAS as the highest decision making body.[48] This is further complicated by the fact that other provisions of the treaty confer extensive powers upon the new Mediation and Security Council (MSC) to which the Authority has delegated all its powers: "Without prejudice to its wide-ranging powers under Article 9 of the Treaty and Article 6 above, the authority hereby mandates the Mediation and Security Council to take on its behalf appropriate decisions for the implementation of the provisions of this mechanism."[49] The MSC is the body primarily responsible for peace and security within the sub-region. Pursuant to the provisions of Article 7, it has a wide range of powers enabling it to decide on all matters relating to peace and security. Not only can the MSC decide appropriate policies on conflict prevention or resolution, but it can also authorize all forms of intervention and decide, in particular on the deployment of political and military missions, approve mandates and terms of reference for such missions and review them periodically on the basis of evolving situations.[50]

These dispositions conflict with other dispositions and principles of the Charter. International peace and security is the *domaine réservé* of the Council and although retroactive legalization has been argued, interventions by regional organizations still require prior UN Security Council authorization. After several discussions in Banjul, and in New York on 29 April, 2002, ECOWAS officials, through the executive secretary of ECOWAS, Mohammed Ibn Chambas, finally determined that, based on the extreme reluctance of the Security Council to sanction or authorize UN missions in Liberia and Sierra Leone, it would be better to retain autonomy over the decision to intervene, and not to let the UN Security Council, given its unwillingness to intervene, prevent ECOWAS from taking urgent action to maintain sub-regional stability.[51] The implications of article 10 (c) of the Mechanism empowering the MSC to "authorize all forms of intervention and decide particularly on the deployment of political and military missions" are numerous because, once again, the treaty does not appear to appreciate the distinctions between classical peacekeeping, peace enforcement actions and humanitarian intervention. These problems need to be addressed.

CONFLICT OF NORMS

Whereas regional organizations and agencies are not precluded from undertaking actions related to peace within their respective regions,[52] they are prohibited from initiating enforcement actions without the prior authorization of the Security Council.[53]

Clearly Article 10 of the treaty raises concern when it is recalled that Article 22 (c) includes humanitarian intervention in the list of actions that ECOMOG may regulate under the Mechanism. Regional arrangements have lately circumvented the requirements of Article 53 (1) of the UN Charter by acting first and later seeking legitimation from the Security Council.[54] This practice, however, does not nullify the requirement that still legally exits in the Charter. Within the confines of international law, any obligations of the ECOWAS members belonging to the UN which conflict with the obligations imposed by the UN Charter are void. [55] The Charter has a higher rank, and the obligations derived from the Charter must prevail over ECOWAS dispositions when the two conflict. Indeed the UN Charter places a great emphasis on the peaceful settlement of disputes and the principle of non-use of force. The new treaty, which empowers member states to use force without the authorization of the Security Council contravenes the peremptory norm of international law contained in Articles 2 (4) and 103 of the UN Charter. These must prevail because with the adoption of the UN Charter states have surrendered to the Security Council their rights to determine and use force against other states. They retain it exceptionally, i.e., only in case of individual and collective self-defense,[56] and they may not undertake forcible actions without its authorization.[57] Therefore, the provisions of article 10 (c) conflicts with the obligations imposed on ECOWAS member states.

The UN Security Council, for political reasons, has a large scope of discretion on that matter. In exercising its duty, based more on political considerations than on strict law, the Council is free to decide whether and how to use force, but it is also at liberty to determine when to do so. The Charter gives *carte blanche* to the Security Council in evaluating any given situation. Nowhere is the Security Council under fewer strictures than in its obligation to determine whether a threat exists or not.[58] In short, a threat to the peace, in the sense of Article 39 seems to be whatever the Security Council says it is.[59] "It is completely within the discretion of the Security Council to decide what constitutes a threat to the peace."[60] Just as the Security Council may take action against a threat to the peace that is imperceptible, as in Haiti, it may also decline to acknowledge the existence of a manifest threat to the peace, as in Liberia. Scholars often forget that the Security Council is a political, not a judicial organ. Its decisions are linked to political motivations where law is often instrumentalized. As a non-judicial body, the Council is not required to set out reasons for its decisions. But it is very important for the Council to assume its great responsibility. Where the Security Council has the primary responsibility to act, it should do so. Although independent, it is necessary for the Council to mobilize support and avoid situations that would discredit it.

Because the powers of the Security Council are wide, it must exercise them with a sense of responsibility. Legally, politically and morally, the Security Council is required to act on behalf of all member states of the UN and it is on that condition that its wide powers remain valid. Where the Security Council, for instance, fails to take action under any of the provisions listed in Chapters VI, VII, VIII, which are the core of the Purposes and the Principles of the UN, it violates Article 24 and is not legally and morally qualified to prevent a sub-regional organization such as ECOWAS from doing so. The council is not perceived as a true representative of the international community and following the ECOWAS intervention, considerable views and numerous voices insisted on the rightfulness for states to reclaim the previously transferred responsibility for collective security to the regional organs because of the Security Council's reluctance to intervene.

These criticisms are valid and are grounded on the lack of the fulfillment of the conditions upon which the Security Council was entrusted with that responsibility. This has been the main reason ECOWAS gave in support of Article 10. Although regional organizations appreciate the importance of their obligations under the United Nations Charter, recent examples in Africa have shown that the cost of waiting for the United Nations authorization could be very high in terms of life and resources. The Council is not considered as upholding the interests of all states, and should act in a fashion to correct it. Here an example must suffice: an action taken by ECOWAS, which meets all the conditions of necessity, does not qualify to be taken on behalf of the international community but an action taken or authorized by the five permanent members of the Security Council, even in the face of opposition by the majority of the General Assembly, is the only one so certified.

The UN Charter is binding on all member states, and indeed on the Security Council itself. After all, the Charter charges the Council with the primary responsibility for the maintenance of international peace and security. Article 39 employs the mandatory expression "shall" to describe the Council's task. The Council "shall" determine the existence of a threat to the peace, and a breach to the peace, and "shall" either make recommendations or decide what is to be done. For several reasons, the interests of the powerful nations being the supreme, the Council may be reluctant to intervene. In such a case, the political bargaining should not prevent other organizations willing to preserve peace and order to do so. The determination that a threat exists, due to its importance, is not a totally discretionary one, and has to remain within the limits of the Purposes and Principles of the Charter. In other words, the Security Council has no right to place itself above the most important rule of international society. The

Report of the International Commission on Intervention and State Sovereignty takes the same view. The commission agrees that there is no better or more appropriate body than the United Nations Security Council to authorize military intervention for human protection purposes. It further stresses that any effort to justify military intervention without Security Council's authorization remains highly contentious.[61] Finally, the report concluded that the issue is not so much finding an alternative to the Security Council as a source of authority, but making the Council work better than it does. The Commission insisted on the obligation of the Security Council to deal promptly with any request for authority to intervene where there are allegations of large-scale loss of human life and ethnic cleansing. It is envisioned that, when the Security Council rejects a proposal or fails to deal with it within a reasonable time, two options remain: the procedure under "Uniting for Peace" by the General Assembly or, as in the case of ECOWAS, an action by the concerned states in order to meet the gravity and urgency of the situation.

In this chapter it has been pointed out that ECOMOG encountered many difficulties in Liberia. The West African force faced the problems of political unity, the capacity to assure effective execution of the many agreements signed, not to mention the logistical limitations of its soldiers who lacked the equipment and intelligence required for counterinsurgency in Liberia. Even the lack of the means of communications poses a great problem. These difficulties are not resolved by the adoption of a New Security Mechanism. The adoption of the "African Solutions to African Problems" position needs to be implemented, not only to be declared. The decentralization of peace operations to the regional body is intended to facilitate that goal. But a series of limits, difficulties and even risks that this entails will be examined in the next chapter remain.

Chapter Five

Regional Approach: Speculations and Realities

The idea of making greater use of regional arrangements has been revisited at the United Nations in the 1990s with the publication of an *Agenda for Peace* which received renewed attention with the international debate that accompanied NATO intervention in Kosovo, not authorized by the Security Council. During the debate on the NATO intervention, African experiences were not mentioned as precedents, which may have been a sign of the pervasive lack of attention paid to events in Africa. The objective of this chapter is to discuss the regional approach in the West African context. It is argued that except for some mentions of the concept, this doctrine does not yet exist. Furthermore, in West Africa, the rivalry between "Anglophone" and "Francophone" countries, the external reliance on foreign support, and the institutional weaknesses of the countries constitute challenges to that seemingly attractive approach.

THE ORIGINS OF THE DEBATE

After the end of the Cold War and the coalition campaign to liberate Kuwait, a new era was said to have arrived in which the UN would be able to deal with international peace and security. Following that euphoria the Secretary General undertook the preparation of a report intended to propose ideas and strategies on how to enhance the capacity of the international organization on that fundamental matter. Revisiting what had been his doctoral dissertation,[1] the then Secretary General Boutros Boutros-Ghali insisted on the potential for regional organizations to contribute to peace operations. The Secretary General perceived their role as a matter of decentralization, delegation and cooperation with the objective of lightening the burden of the Security Council, which would contribute to a deeper sense of participation, consensus and democratization in international affairs. In the Secretary's General view, such efforts would have positive results. He estimated that consultations between the United Nations and regional bodies "could do much to build international consensus on the nature of a problem and the measures required to address it. Regional organizations participating in complementary efforts with the United Nations in joint undertakings would encourage states outside the region to act supportively."[2]

Although briefly discussed in 1995, the debate on Africa started in the Security Council in September 1997 by the Foreign Ministers with the objective of addressing and preventing conflicts on the continent.[3] A Presidential Statement, exclusively focused on Africa, noted that "the challenges in Africa demand a more comprehensive response" and requested the Secretary General to submit recommendations on ways to address and prevent conflicts in Africa and to establish a foundation of peace on the continent.[4] The Secretary General's report of 1998 was, however, disappointing because it did not contain any doctrine on the relationship between regional organizations and the United Nations, but just a general unspecified answer on how to deal with African conflicts. Nothing was new in the report; it just restated that Africa needed more attention:

> By not averting these colossal human tragedies, African leaders have failed the peoples of Africa; the international community has failed them; the United Nations has failed them. We have failed them by not adequately addressing the causes of conflicts; by not doing enough to ensure peace; and by our repeated inability to create the conditions of sustainable development.[5]

This is the sort of empty statement that may contribute to discrediting the roles of international organizations because development is not an obligation to be carried out by international organizations. Nowhere does this responsibility exist. On the contrary it is the responsibility of each nation to take the necessary national initiatives to foster its own development. The society of states can probably assist these efforts in a variety of ways, but the responsibility falls primarily on the shoulders of the leaders of these nations.

Further discussions and meetings were held in 1999; presidential statements and reports continued to be issued but these documents did not put forth new proposals that set a comprehensive approach to or a new model of cooperation between the UN and regional arrangements.[6] Instead, they restated well-known facts such as the new task poses "considerable challenges," that it needs "financial and logistical resources,"[7] and that the international community's commitment to dealing with conflict must be applied fairly and consistently, irrespective of region.[8] During the "Month of Africa" at the Security Council in 1999, African speakers at the UN echoed the same views, and expressed a high level of frustration regarding the disparity in the international community's responses to crises in Africa and elsewhere.[9] The meetings on the roles of regional organizations were more a forum of protest where delegates expressed their disappointment rather than a place where concrete proposals were elaborated. The discussions revolved around the marginalization and neglect of the African continent, the need for political commitment and sufficient will, but nothing new emerged.

Although ECOWAS was the first regional organization to intervene in a conflict without Security Council authorization, it was NATO's involvement in the Balkans that actually drew more attention to the role of regional organizations in situations of humanitarian crises. Following both the intervention in Kosovo and the previous UN failures in Bosnia and in other places in Africa, the Secretary General established an independent panel to examine a new UN approach to peace operations with the stated objectives of enhancing the credibility of the international organization. The panel, chaired by Lakhdar Brahimi, a former Algerian Foreign Minister, included members from all continents and issued its report in 2000. The report covered a wide range of issues such as preventive action, peace-building strategy, strategic analysis, military personnel, mission leadership, logistical support, management, operational support, rapidly deployable forces. A catalogue of well-known facts was raised, as well as had been in previous studies, such as "clear, credible and achievable mandates," "necessity to act before the crisis degenerates," "commitment of Member States to provide political, material and financial support . . ."

The *raison d'être* of the mission was to draft "a new approach" but it only covered a range of practical and other technical issues, already recognized in UN circles and remained extremely modest on its mission. In its seventy pages, the report provided only one paragraph on the question. It made a vague reference to and endorsed the concept of regional approach without providing any further comment or proposals, as shown by the following paragraph:

> The Charter clearly encourages cooperation with regional and subre-
> gional organizations to resolve conflicts and establish and maintain

peace and security. The United Nations is actively and successfully engaged in many such cooperation programmes in the field of conflict prevention, peacemaking, elections and electoral assistance, human rights monitoring and humanitarian work, and other peacebuilding activities in various parts of the world. Where peacekeeping operations are concerned, however, caution seems appropriate, because military resources and capability are unevenly distributed around the world, and troops in the most crisis-prone areas are often less prepared for the demands of peacekeeping than is the case elsewhere. Providing training, equipment, logistical support and other resources to regional organizations could enable peacekeepers from all regions to participate in a United Nations peacekeeping operation or to set up regional peacekeeping operations on the basis of a Security Council resolution.[10]

Given the extensive and detailed nature of the report, this was a very limited acknowledgment of the role of regional organizations. It did not address the problem of the legality of operations undertaken by regional organizations without the Security Council's authorization. Both in Liberia and in Kosovo, the regional organizations acted without a Security Council authorization, and the extent to which these operations were legal was widely and hotly debated at that time. The lack of attention to the problem of unauthorized intervention, in contrast to the extensive international debate at the time, is surprising. According to the model contained in the UN Charter, institutional cooperation is conceived through the Security Council authorizing the operation, and delegating in the same or separate decision, the regional organization to undertake the authorized tasks. Such cooperation is based on the primacy of the United Nations Charter and on the role of the Security Council as the only entity with the power to authorize the use of force.[11] This is what international law requires, although events in Liberia, Kosovo and Sierra Leone have followed a different sequence.

Finally, the lack of serious examination of the so-called regional approach is reflected in the undifferentiated perspective the report applied to the concept of region. Drafting a concept and a set of rules and principles that apply to both ECOWAS and NATO is like comparing apples and oranges. ECOWAS and NATO have few things in common. All that NATO needs is the blessing of the UN and the subsequent legitimatization of its action in order to gain political acceptability. After that it can do the heavy lifting and does not need the United Nations. It could probably do the job better than the UN. For ECOWAS the situation is different. It needs the UN and the international community's determination and willingness to commit resources. Therefore, if such commitment is the key for success, ECOWAS is a dependent organization. While NATO does not need a checklist, ECOWAS will require everything from uniforms to communication equipment, transport, medical, and other basic supplies. NATO needs the umbrella of the Security Council; ECOWAS needs the requisite logistical, financial and material support. The greatest obstacle for a regionally led intervention in Africa is the inability of its members to face these challenges.

REGIONAL INTERVENTION AS CAPACITY

State incapacity owing to a widespread poverty and underdevelopment is the biggest problem of West African states.

The Brahimi Report recommended that the international community should provide for logistical and financial support, the training of specialized troops, larger units of soldiers, and better equipment. In fact, one may assume that these basic requirements were not written for NATO but solely in the light of ECOMOG's problems in performing its duties in Liberia and in Sierra Leone. At the present time, it is not realistic to argue that ECOWAS members can provide solutions to ECOMOG's resource constraints because among the fifteen ECOWAS states, almost all are bankrupt and grinding poverty is the nightmare of their citizens. By 1997, only three states (Bénin, Côte d'Ivoire, and Nigeria) had paid their contributions to ECOWAS in full,[12] and the situation is not getting better. For budgetary reasons, the move of the ECOWAS secretariat from Lagos to Abuja was delayed by seven years and its staff is irregularly paid, due to lack of funds.[13] In this situation, having new desk officers to monitor human rights violations, cross-border crime, circulation of light arms and drug control, as envisaged by the New Security Mechanism, was an unrealistic proposal. These problems are not resolved by the adoption of constitutions.

The point that I am making is not about the irrelevance of the idea of regional integration or cooperation. There is no doubt that a number of issues are better dealt with through regional cooperation. But the states are the core of the region. What are the chances of success of an organization whose membership is composed mostly of collapsed and collapsing states? Is it not more realistic to have functioning states first before moving forward? If the leaders did not succeed in managing smaller units (the states), is there any reason to be optimistic on a higher level? The absence of ordered, capable and credible states is the first challenge for ECOWAS, and until that equation finds a solution, the idea of regionalism will be at best a work in progress. Regional integration starts by the building of functioning states and most of these states are elusive in West Africa.

At the operational level, advocates of the regional approach argue that geographical proximity is an advantage. They often seem to forget that West Africa is ethnically, linguistically and culturally diverse. Regional soldiers can be ignorant of the realities of even a neighboring country. Supporters of the regional approach assume also that proximity to the conflict creates an immediate interest for regional forces to find a solution to the conflict. This was not true of Liberia. Some states agreed to send troops later, after the conflict, while others withdrew from a prolonged war. In terms of capacity, ECOWAS has little experience and lacks technical capabilities. A conventionally well-trained force is preferable to an indigenous irregular and inexperienced force. Temporary coalitions and other *ad hoc* groupings (such as the SMC set up at the request of Babangida) should limit their mandate to that of peacekeeping and diplomacy. Finally, one must recognize that the concept of region in West Africa is an empty reference. Historically, the call for unity was only a populist reaction of individual states resisting neo-imperialism in the wake of decolonization. Consequently, the weakness of the states translated into a weakness of the region in many ways.[14]

West African states are not able to control their territories and borders. The economy of the countries is dependent on foreign subsidies and investments and national production cannot cover the basic needs of the populations. Despite the rhetoric, these governments have little choice but to accept the policies imposed by International Financial Institutions (IFIs) of the World Bank and the International Monetary Fund (IMF). West African countries continue to receive strict instructions on how to govern and cannot announce a national budget to their people without the agents of economic colonialism. African leaders still believe that institutions such as the IMF or the World Bank or the World Trade Organization (WTO) are Samaritans set up to help Africa. The exploitation of African economies still continues in a form of neo-exploitation because their economies are controlled from outside. Most of the leaders spent their times traveling in European and other capitals and then afterwards announce to their populations the results of their visits with the naïve certitude that outside decisions and foreign recommendations will save and modernize their economies. These parasitic governments continue to borrow money that they will never be able to repay while the living standards of their citizens are falling drastically.

These problems need to be resolved; otherwise they will continue to adversely affect the capacity of the region. To overcome them, concrete actions and hard work are needed in lieu of solemn commitments during anniversaries and other commemorations. The state is a prerequisite to the region, and regional integration in whatever form is subordinate to the existence of functioning states that will carry national projects. Regional integration is not the end of national responsibility. The problems of African states are known and have been identified in a plethora of plans and programs of actions. What is needed is not more plans, more constitutions, or a new expertise, but more commitment on the part of leaders, as negatively evidenced in Liberia, Guinea, Côte d'Ivoire and in other places where the leaders showed little capability, interest, cooperation and capacity in dealing with the conflicts.[15] The biggest problem in West African politics is the absence of enlightened leaders who have political will. What is needed are concrete actions to fill the socio-economic void, a political environment to guarantee human rights, the observance of the rule of law, moral probity, and accountability on the part of those who hold public offices. What is in place is the daily instrumentalization of constitutions on the part of those who hold power.[16] African leaders need to commit themselves to the basic functions of government necessary for the ameliorations that their citizens have been waiting for since the days of independence. These demands cannot be eternally deferred and their solutions are not in grandiose and enthusiastic regional meetings. Besides the problems related to effective regional cooperation and domestic vitality, the problem of leadership at the regional level is also salient.

THE PROBLEM OF HEGEMONY

In previous chapters Nigeria's role in providing the overwhelming majority of the forces in Liberia was outlined. The country demonstrated its indispensability by contributing between 75 and 80 percent of the ECOMOG forces.[17] There is no doubt that Nigeria has played a crucial role, and no other country in West Africa has such capacity. Is that enough to be an effective hegemon? Do other states accept Nigeria's pretentious stature as the hegemonic power and do they deal with it?

Without underestimating Nigeria's role, the extent to which it shaped the outcomes of the conflict is unclear at all levels. While Nigeria was seeking a solution to the conflict in Liberia, it was also the problem. Despite the lack of commitment to peace by the different factions and the violations of the accords signed under ECOWAS auspices, Nigeria's involvement did not offer much guarantee of a successful intervention. The first problem was the lack of neutrality. From the beginning, Nigeria saw the intervention as a war against Charles Taylor, the main warlord. Taylor's forces expressed their doubts about Nigeria on several occasions, and during each negotiating session repeatedly demanded that Nigerian forces be reduced, because Nigeria was hostile to the NPFL.[18] Although Nigeria's objective was to prevent Taylor from becoming president, it did not succeed. Neutrality is the cornerstone of successful mediation. Not only must mediators be fair but also they need to be perceived as such by all parties. That lack of objectivity has also been denounced by other ECOWAS members. It has been reported that Sénégalese and Togolese diplomats and other officials could not understand General Babangida's excessive interest in who became Liberia's president after the ECOWAS mediation: "Taylor's integrity is in serious doubt, but so is the integrity of Nigeria's leaders. Besides, if the process we are negotiating produces Taylor as Liberia's leader, why should we not accept it?"[19] This reservation is not only an expression of what has been called the "Francophone dimension" of the ECOWAS intervention.[20] Ghana expressed similar misgivings. Yet its association with Nigeria remained to be explained.

The states in the region were indeed divided, but Nigeria was unable to unite them and to exercise leadership over them for a common objective. A hegemon should be able to influence the other member states in the region, but Nigeria was not decisive in taking a clear position of influence and leadership *vis-à-vis* the other members of the community because of its own internal disorder and disunity. Although Sierra Leone was very close to Nigeria, two main factors can justify that proximity. The country was receiving aid from Nigeria and at the same time was in conflict with Taylor, for its own reasons because his troops were backing a rebel group in Sierra Leone that was endangering the government. Despite disagreements with Nigeria, Sierra Leone could not withdraw because Taylor supported its internal rebellion.

In addition to its contested leadership at the regional level, Nigeria also faced domestic opposition. At the beginning of 1994, the country reached the point of donor fatigue and one observer noted that:

> Despite its dedication to ECOMOG Nigeria also reached a point where it began to reexamine its involvement and commitment to the operation. This was evident in an emerging ambivalence about the presence of Nigerian troops in Liberia. Before the November 1993 military coup in Nigeria, the head of the Interim National Government, Chief Ernest Shonekan, announced plans to withdraw Nigerian troops from ECO-MOG.[21]

As is the case in many countries, public opinion cannot support hazardous operations that divert money away from domestic areas in desperate need of funding. Domestic protest was decisive in Nigeria and it has been reported that internal opposition and popular demonstrations caused more damage than regional insecurity.[22] Its domestic political process suffered a blow from its involvement in Liberia and one can imagine the skepticism of Nigerian citizens and the difficulties of convincing them of the urgency of bringing the Liberian factions to the negotiating table and forcing them to organize elections. After all were not Nigerians themselves waiting for the same thing in the country? There is something ironic to invest all of one's energy in the organization of elections in Liberia while stifling the same process at home. Nigeria could not convince the factions on the argument on democracy either. Doubts were justified by their inability to practice it at home.[23] The denial to its own community of these rights is a powerful argument that both factions and citizens at home used. Certainly, this does not increase the international status of the hegemon, but fairly opens it more to criticism. In addition to these already complicated problems, the region is also facing a political divide between anglophone and francophone countries.

HERITAGE AND PERPETUATION OF REGIONAL DIVIDE

President François Mitterrand noted once: "Without Africa, France will no longer have a history in the twenty-first century."[24] President Georges Pompidou expressed the same concern on a state visit in Africa and declared: "The French-speaking countries should harmonize their views and coordinate their efforts, vis-à-vis English-speaking Africa and Nigeria in particular."[25] Pompidou's visit accelerated the creation of the CEAO, which was originally intended to strengthen the French-speaking countries and to contain Nigeria's influence in West Africa.

The CEAO was an insurance against its aspirations and to this date, Francophone countries have more ties with France than with Nigeria. They pay more attention to Paris than to Abuja. France has official and unofficial networks that Nigeria does not have. It maintains a politico-military presence in the form of bases, forces and militarily defense agreements. These accords, signed with those Francophone African countries considered to be the most important for France, cover the supply of weapons, the training of army officers, the formation of police forces, secret services, intelligence agencies, presidential guards, and when needed, military intervention to ensure the *status quo*.[26] In exchange for these services, France has a permanent and a monopolistic access to minerals, raw materials such oil, natural gas, and uranium. These materials, vital to high-technology industries, have to be sold to France in priority and are restricted for other countries.[27]

At the level of higher education and research, several agencies are responsible for carrying out French programs whose *coopérants* provide technical assistance in schools and universities. Several missions coordinate exchanges among members, universities, institutes and centers. Since the end of the 1990s, African universities have been places of insurrection and protest and many West African scholars are attracted by European and North American universities because inter-African exchange programs are weak. In fact, there are little opportunities for inter-African exchange programs. In national programs, Sénégalese students study more about France than they do about Nigeria. In short, France has developed channels in order to maintain power over former colonies and to continue economic, political and cultural policies and sustain an important place in the world, despite its weaknesses in some sectors. France needs international organizations and its ex-colonies to maintain its aspirations and carry its visions of the world.

In the mid 1990s that presence has been reinforced at the intergovernmental cooperation level through the revitalization of the Francophonie. Initiated for the promotion of linguistic programs, the Francophonie, as evidenced since the summits of Hanoi (1997), Moncton (1999) and Beirut (2002), has developed a political role, which revolves around the promotion of the rule of law and the strengthening of democracy within the Francophone community. In November 2000, it adopted an important declaration, referred to as the Bamako Declaration, which gives the Community common benchmarks for democracy and human rights. It also provides for mechanisms to prevent crises in democracy, and for measures to be taken in case of massive violations of human rights. It has since been translated into a draft program of action to be undertaken by the Francophone agencies to support training for members of national legal services, consolidation of legal institutions and support for election processes. Francophone states retain their closest ties with the former colonial power rather than with Nigeria, and preserve common institutions inherited at independence. In short, the Francophonie has a desire to play an important role as "political stabilizer" in Francophone Africa, in preventing conflict, consolidating efforts to democratize and instill good governance as well as in encouraging respect for human rights. More specifically, France's commitment to multilateralism demonstrates the country's willingness to openly show the world its vision. This involvement also enables France to strengthen its bilateral and multilateral relations and to consolidate its objectives in the areas of peace, development, cooperation and its message.

This will be a fundamental challenge for Nigeria's search for hegemony in West Africa. It will also manifest itself in the resolution of conflicts such as in Côte d'Ivoire. The conflict challenged the concept of regional approach as well as the decision of the United Nations to establish the West African office, with the objective of promoting the new regional approach through the strengthening of the partnership between ECOWAS and the UN. On September 19, 2002 a rebellion started in Côte d'Ivoire when a group of soldiers and a dissident general, Robert Gueï, protested against having been demobilized by the incumbent president, Laurent Gbagbo. Just as in Liberia, nobody believed that the situation would be complicated and all assumed that the rebels would be easily defeated. But it appeared that the rebels, who have been part of the army and know its weaknesses, were as well armed as the loyalists.[28] They soon carried out a level of violence and savagery from an earlier stage. ECOWAS engaged in diplomatic initiatives to solve the conflict, but it did not accomplish much. The majority of the leaders in the region did not even try, as evidenced by the fact that only three heads of states attended the Dakar summit devoted to the problem.[29] The cease-fire agreement signed on October 17, 2002, under the mediation of President Abdoulaye Wade of Sénégal who at that time was the chairman of ECOWAS, and the subsequent peace talks held in Lomé, Togo, under the mediation of President Gnassingbe Eyadema in his capacity as mediator of the Francophonie, were violated even before the ink had dried on the documents, and the problems of leadership and rivalry developed between the two leaders.[30]

France's motivations for having a mediator drawn from the ranks of Francophonie were in part the result of its interests in the conflict. Finally, both leaders failed and, following the ECOWAS fiasco, French foreign minister, Dominique de Villepin, embarked on a visit to West Africa after which he obtained a cease-fire.[31] He later relocated the negotiations in Paris, after weeks of deadlock in Togo had confirmed the West African leaders' inability to work together and to come up with a settlement proposal.[32] This event is one of the many examples that illustrates in West Africa the dependence of the states and the fact that the regional idea is far from reality. France has interests in Côte d'Ivoire (one of the world's top cocoa producers and the region's second largest economy after Nigeria). Anyone familiar with the "geopolitics" of the region could have predicted that France would not leave the initiative to Nigeria or to any other country. Not only Nigeria but also ECOWAS itself played a marginal role during the crisis, and when the African leaders met on February 10, 2003 in the Ivorian capital, it was not to discuss the peace process, but the post 'Marcoussis Accord,' which referred to the agreement concluded on January 24 in Linas-Marcoussis, France. These did not also produce much result and success and ECOWAS in fact tried to revitalize them on several occasions with no tangible effect.

SOVEREIGNTY AGAIN?

There are too many challenges to the new UN approach to decentralizing peace operations to regional bodies as the African never-ending wars illustrate. In light of the Brahimi report examined previously, the UN Secretary General dispatched an Inter-Agency Mission to West Africa, led by Ibrahima Fall, then Assistant Secretary General for Political Affairs, to visit the countries of the region in order "to take stock of the priority needs and challenges and make recommendations on a coordinated United Nations response to the multifaceted problems confronting the region."[33]

The report presented a complete picture of the political dynamics as well as the regional actors involved in manipulating the conflicts, notably the alliances among armed groups within the region.[34] It raised a number of issues concerning conflict prevention, peacekeeping, peacebuilding, disarmament, implementation of sanctions, humanitarian assistance, refugees, human rights, and good governance. It also stressed the point that economic development and regional integration should constitute important elements of a sub-regional approach. In addition, it argued that a comprehensive sub-regional strategy and mechanism of implementation was needed, and finally made the recommendation that the United Nations should establish an office in West Africa in order to intensify collaboration between the United Nations system and ECOWAS. It insisted that the international community "should consider the strengthening of ECOWAS and support efforts to create a framework for integration," "provide for capacity building of ECOWAS secretariat and enhance mechanisms dealing with conflict prevention, the judiciary and human rights . . ."[35]

Once again, the main flaw of the report and the whole idea of a new approach for peace and security in West Africa is that the roles of these countries were not emphasized as they should, and the responsibility of the international community was overestimated. Is it realistic to place such responsibility on the international community? Is it realistic to think that the countries called upon to embark on this direction will finance it? I realistically think they will continue to fulfill the obligations of their own constituencies first, and indeed, the primary responsibility of a leader is toward its citizens. If real progress is to be made in supporting regional military groupings as its proponents propose, the developed countries will need to divert very substantial resources from their domestic sector. But I am not certain that western leaders are ready to take that considerable political risk, despite rhetorical commitment, unless there are realistic prospects for national gain from taking such actions.

Primarily responsible for insecurity in West Africa are the leaders who sponsor armed groups to operate in other member states. Respect for the principle of non-intervention is a good beginning. This is by far the most important problem, which does not need a new rule, or a new treaty; what it does need is respect for existing rules and practices. The state sponsored violence in West Africa will be resolved not only by the adoption of a new mechanism, the opening of a new office but by responsible behavior on the part of the leaders engaged on these operations. After Liberia, Sierra Leone and Guinea, it has been claimed that Ghana got involved in the crisis in Côte d'Ivoire and that Burkina Faso once again, supported rebel groups to settle accounts with Côte d'Ivoire.[36] These leaders must respect the principle of non-interference in the domestic affairs of other states. Without that obedience there will be no stability in the region. In fact, these problems are not complicated at all. It is the responsibility of the elites and the leaders to work for peace by beginning to take responsibility for the harmful activities of piracy and mercenarism, and other violent actions that emanate from their citizens, their armed group rebels, or territories.

Member states that supported Charles Taylor continuously violated UN resolutions and embargos on the importation of arms for a decade, and continue as well to provide sanctuary for armed groups, to threaten and destabilize neighboring countries.[37] The same support of rebels continues to develop in the region. According to the National Party of Côte d'Ivoire press, Blaise Compaoré, is supporting the rebellion in their country. The animosity with which Compaoré once described president Gbagbo of Côte d'Ivoire may have validated that suspicion. During the negotiations for the peace process in France, he urged president Laurent Gbagbo to step down: "in the long term the only solution to the crisis in his country is for Gbagbo to go." He accused president Laurent Gbagbo of having committed numerous atrocities and predicted that his destiny would be similar to that of Slobodan Milosevic who is on trial at the International Criminal Tribunal for his actions in the former Yugoslavia.[38] But the president of Burkina Faso forgot that he himself came to power after having assassinated his best friend, former president Thomas Sankara.

It seems that the UN did not fully evaluate the risk of the regional approach due to the geopolitics of the region and the hostilities described below. Better judgment and caution are needed. The issue at stake is not the relevance of regional organizations, but what tasks should be devolved to them at the present time. It is not suitable to give to regimes that are hostile to their neighbors a right to intervene without Security Council approval, and probably even with Security Council approval. Many of the regimes that might intervene are themselves engaged in barbarous acts, thus their interventions may generate problems for an unfriendly regime. The regional approach may lead to peace, but intervention also means guns in the hands of the leaders and this can lead to unforeseen consequences. Is it not grotesque to give dictators *carte blanche* to intervene in other states for the promotion of a democratic regime? This is not democracy but the extension of tyranny beyond its borders. Law without justice is tyranny. The risk exists of regional inter-state clashes being more destabilizing than the violations of human rights they seek to correct. If one has to choose between the promotion of justice or human rights in Liberia, Guinea or in any other country, and peace security and stability for the whole region, the latter is preferable.

The reality is that unjust and undemocratic regimes, as like almost all in West Africa, cannot promote justice in another country. The international status of a mediating power in a conflict is important. An undemocratic leader cannot convince countries that are involved in hostilities to resolve their disputes by democratic means. It will not help them because it does not have the expertise and the tradition of such bargaining. The later president of Togo was the mediator in the crisis in Côte d'Ivoire, but it was not a good idea because, just a few weeks before mediating the crisis in Cote d'Ivoire, president Eyadéma had modified article 59 of the Constitution to allow him to run for office again although he could not do so under the previous constitution. Does it make sense to appoint a head of state to mediate in a conflict on the basis of democratic principles when he himself did not adhere to those principles? Does such a mediator have any chance of success?

There is a school of thought that blames the violations of African constitutions on the *mimétisme constitutionnel,* i.e., on the fact that these constitutions were copied from Western models, which may explain the difficulties in respecting these norms. But the problem lies elsewhere. It is not necessarily the imported nature of those documents but rather that the elites who are not committed to adhering to these provisions. All African constitutions have prescriptions on elective institutions, separation of powers and governmental responsibilities. The problem is that they are not followed. Togo is not the only example. In most of these countries, opponents have been threatened and jailed, often at the time of elections. There is a risk that regional politics in Africa will be merely the continuation of domestic politics. In order for Nigeria or for any other West African states to fulfill its regional ambitions, it needs to provide more than military power or rhetoric. It needs to be stable and, on the premise that charity begins at home, resolve its internal problems and the widespread demands of its citizens. I am not however implying that if a hegemonic power is truly virtuous, it would have the right to intervene.

Finally, the regional approach critically examined appears to be an unwanted responsibility, an option by default. Since Africa has lost its geostrategic interest, major powers do not want to commit resources. By following without discernment the rhetoric of regionalization, African leaders are giving to the Security Council, which is already reluctant to support peace operations, the opportunity for disengaging from African conflicts, because it is clear that the main powers will no longer police crises in which their national interests are not at risk. In an *Agenda for Peace,* regional organizations were perceived as a means to lighten the burden; now they seek means to disengage from African affairs. Since the experiences of Somalia and Rwanda, little has changed in the international commitment toward African conflicts. In the face of numerous tensions and hostility among leaders, the Security Council's central responsibility for the maintenance of international peace and security must be reaffirmed to avoid the risk of the use of force in situations that are legally wrong and morally indefensible. The circumstances justifying the use of force against a sovereign country are extremely restricted. Following its intervention in Liberia, ECOMOG initiated similar actions in Sierra Leone and in Guinea, gaining a greater independence of action that may ultimately have negative effects.

The conflict in Côte d'Ivoire challenged all the constructions that were said to offer solutions to African conflicts. ECOWAS has a new mechanism for security; and the UN, in the aftermath of the recommendations of the Inter-Agency Mission, has an office in Dakar to support ECOWAS and enhance the UN capacity. The result of their involvement in the crisis is so far disappointing. Their initiatives repeatedly failed. Unless the great powers have an interest in a crisis, it remains to be seen if they will support the regional approach. The problems are so multifaceted, the demands so appalling, peace operations so expensive that no one wants that responsibility. What does this imply for West African states? What should they do? What are their responsibilities? In order to reduce the tensions and the crises, the first priority for West African leaders is not to justify humanitarian intervention or to legalize it, but to find ways and means to strengthen state capacity in order for nationals to live in a stable political and social milieu. The first responsibility and objective for African states must be to take the necessary steps to ensure that local grievances do not become a source of internal conflicts that explode at the regional and international level. The first supplier of justice to its citizens is the state, provided the domestic meaning and aspects of sovereignty are understood. These questions will be dealt with in the next chapter.

Chapter Six
Government Legitimacy Versus Humanitarian Intervention

The prevention of human rights violations and deadly conflicts is first and foremost the responsibility of sovereign states. The need of government legitimacy working to achieve fairer distribution of resources throughout society is the highest priority for ECOWAS states. Embracing the concept of humanitarian intervention will not achieve that. The direct causes of African conflicts are due to an ignorance of democratic and constitutional rule, corruption, weak leadership, unaccountability in the use of natural resources. Sovereign states, the communities and institutions within them, need to address the real causes of these conflicts.

SEARCHING FOR THE STATE: FROM COLONIZATION TO MILITARY RULE

Analysts and scholars situate the origins of the Liberian war to the 150 years of the Americo-Liberian administration of the country.[1] Although a number of African scholars adopt that view, I will focus my analysis on the proximate causes of the war. The absence of a functioning state based on a contract of reciprocity between the citizens and the ruling elite has been a main feature in Liberian politics. The country has moved from its peculiar form of colonization to a military coup and did not experience a viable state in which citizens determined their affairs on their own. The country came into existence when, in 1822, some Americans of African decent arrived in Liberia with the nineteenth century ideological and political ideas that emphasized the "civilizing mission." It was said that the natives could not govern themselves and that they lacked the most basic conditions of "civilized" life. Anthony Daniel expresses this view when he writes:

> The redemption of Africa from the deep degradation, superstition and idolatry in which she has so long been involved . . . lay on our shoulders. The Gospel . . . is yet to be preached to vast numbers inhabiting this Dark Continent, and I have the highest reason to believe, that it was one of the great objects of the Almighty in establishing these colonies, that they might be the means of introducing civilization and religion among the barbarous nations on this country.[2]

Indigenous peoples were perceived as being "primitive" and "inferior" and the "civilized world" therefore had a moral ground and a humanitarian mission to help these desperate places. Thus, the Americo-Liberians found it perfectly normal to reproduce in Liberia the society and the institutions they had known in the United States.[3] For more than a century, the Americo-Liberians dominated the country's political, economic, and social life, even though they constituted only about five percent of the population. In short, the 133 years rule of the Americo-Liberian oligarchy oppressed and excluded the indigenous inhabitants who were reduced to the conditions of subjects. Indeed in 1931, the League of Nations described Liberia as a "Republic of 12.000 citizens with 1,000,000 subjects."[4]

Some measures addressing the problem of exploitation and misery of the native were undertaken between 1944 and 1980 by presidents William V. S. Tubman and William Tolbert. Their successive tenures did not, however, improve the lives of the indigenous people who continued to suffer exclusion from political life. There was no improvement in their conditions; economic inequality worsened and hostility toward the oligarchy embodied in Americo-Liberian families developed. These tensions were exacerbated in 1980 and in April of the same year, a group of soldiers under the leadership of Master Sergeant Samuel Doe assassinated president Tolbert and annihilated within a week all forms of resistance.

However justified, military coups or any other kinds of unconstitutional means of overtaking political power always warrant a miscarriage of an inchoate nation building process. In search of a popular mandate, the new government alleged to be acting on behalf of Liberians of indigenous origin, the country people whom they claimed to have liberated from 133 years of oligarchical rule. The popularity they enjoyed in its early years soon faced the realities of the Liberian masses. The junta found itself under mounting pressure to satisfy the demands of the population. Doe and his fellow-putschists soon realized that it is easier to overthrow a government than to manage the affairs of a state. The coup leaders and most Liberians had no previous experience in public administration and were unprepared to effectively rule the country. They were obliged to cooperate with the

Americo-Liberian elite they had overthrown and to co-opt a generation of progressive politicians. But, Doe limited the allocation of resources exclusively to his ethnic group and lost the trust of the people. He never succeeded in building a functional state in Liberia; or if he did, it collapsed as basic states institutions were quasi-non-existent.

THE ABSENCE OF FUNCTIONING INSTITUTIONS

To the extent that it existed at all, the Liberian state had been dysfunctional since its creation. Before coming to that point some basic features of the state need to be asserted as the state tends to be taken for granted in the study of Africa. In the Weberian tradition, the state is a set of institutions that legitimately claims control over its territory and citizens, and is capable of performing administrative, legal, coercive and other functions:

> The primary formal characteristics of the modern state are as follows: It possesses an administrative and legal order subject to change by legislation, to which the organized corporate activity of the administrative staff, which is also regulated by legislation, is oriented. This system of order claims binding authority, not only over the members of the states, the citizens, most of whom have obtained membership by birth, but also to a very large extent, over all action taking place in the area of its jurisdiction. It is thus a compulsory association with a territorial basis. Furthermore, today, the use of force is regarded as legitimate only so far as it is either permitted by the state or prescribed by it. . . . The claim of the modern state to monopolize the use of force is as essential as to its character of compulsory jurisdiction and of continuous organization.[5]

Liberia was not a state that provided basic services to the population, but one that was dominated by clans. Liberia was a *de jure* state.[6] The country gained international recognition and sovereignty when a small group of people declared the existence of a republic with a capital based in Monrovia. Liberia was from its inception a state existing under the shadow of American paternalism, run as a quasi-colony or protectorate under a form of indirect rule by the Americo-Liberians and whose economy was owned by US corporations. In fact, in many African countries, the process of state failure started just after independence. Leaders expanded the size of the state with huge and inefficient bureaucracies, and elites were more interested in power consolidation and economic accumulation rather than nation building. Despite its omnipresence, the state was not a promoter of *"l'intérêt général"* but rather the private property of a minority and its clients.[7] The elites did not invest but borrowed heavily; they did not develop an agriculture that could feed their populations. Consequently the situation created a pattern of state dependence, and by the mid-1980s, most of these countries depended on external legitimacy.[8]

Structural-functionalists approach states' actions as a result of responses to societal needs by competing groups. John Foster Dulles summarizes six main functions of the state: functional sovereignty over territory; a political machinery; a superior force to deter violence by enforcing the law upon those who defy it; the capacity of governance with an executive body able to administer the law; judicial machinery to settle disputes in accords with the laws; and the capacity to render basic services so that people are not driven by desperation to ways of violence.[9] These *sine qua non* conditions were not met in Liberia. Leaders approached politics as minority power based, dominated by elites or groups who controlled national resources through networks and corrupt practices. The elite never put in place general policy orientation over the distribution of material and non-material resources. In Liberia, informal procedures for the accumulation of wealth, corruption, sale of resources for the benefit of a group developed instead. The state was a notorious partisan institution in the distribution of resources.

BAD GOVERNANCE AS THE CAUSE OF CONFLICTS

At the beginning of his tenure, Doe surrounded himself with some members of the former Americo-Liberian elite and with some progressive leaders, but they soon became his enemies. Personalizing the power, he and Thomas Quiwonkpa (one of the key actors in the 1980 coup who later became the Commanding General of the Armed Forces) dominated Liberian politics at the early stages. The local press presented them as the strongmen of the revolution.[10] It is difficult, given the very limited education they had, to have a clear sense of what their role would entail. They governed more with rhetoric than a sense of purpose: "We did not come to power to follow in the footsteps of those we overthrew. We came to rebuild our country along progressive lines; power is not for us, it is for the people because if they fail to support us there will be no revolution."[11] Based on his more populist rhetoric, Quiwonkpa's growing popularity became a source of discomfort for Doe. In order to consolidate his power, he transferred Quiwonkpa from the position of Commanding General to that of the Secretary of the PRC. It was an attempt to make it difficult for him to influence the army. But Quiwonkpa refused to be transferred and was dismissed from the force.

Since the so-called revolution, the government and the administrative body were not able to preserve themselves. To complicate matters, the conflict between the two leaders soon translated into hostilities between their respective ethnic groups, i.e., between the Krahn on the one side and the Gio-Mano people on the other. After the split, the state apparatus was used to administer violence on adversaries. To keep their privileges intact, leaders resorted to violence and security was not guaranteed. The state was not a servant of its people but a source of terror, domination and repression for its citizens. Contrary to a system rooted in a tradition of constitutional rule, where the police and military are not permitted to use needless and preventable violence, the state apparatus served to advance the dominance of the Krahn ethnic group over the others. In such a situation, the security of opponents and their families was in danger. Fearing for his life, Quiwonkpa and his close associates went into exile in different countries within the region, principally in Côte d'Ivoire and Ghana. The apparent welcome they received fueled the paranoia of the government in Monrovia who identified "terrorists from abroad" as a major security threat.

The mid-1980s witnessed pressures on the part of great powers on their allies for more political participation. Doe, a close ally of Washington, had to accommodate these external demands. After spending time manipulating institutions and structures that could earn him a victory, he felt safe enough to run for election. In October 1985, he doctored election results and recycled himself from a military man to a civilian.[12] Notwithstanding the dismal record of Doe regime's, Washington maintained close ties with Monrovia for strategic reasons, one being to contain Soviet influence.[13] Ironically, it was the process of meeting external demands that accelerated popular rejection of the regime. Evidently, international pressure cannot bring democracy. The organization of elections alone is not a commitment to greater participation and good governance. At the international level, the rhetoric of "democratic transition" perversely encouraged "democratic manipulation."[14] When a state is not internally legitimate, it is always in a "continual process of crisis management" or in a situation of "politics of survival."[15] At the moment of struggle, the Liberian state violated public liberties, ignored civil and constitutional rights, and if challenged or resisted, was inclined to murder or torture its opponents. In such a situation, repression becomes the dominant instrument of governance.

African conflicts are rarely ethnic in origin. They are manipulated by elites who extend favors to other groups or manipulate divisions when it appears that the leader can no longer depend only on his group. In Liberia repression was associated with the manipulation of ethnic allegiances. Doe, a Krahn, extended favors to the Mandingo community, a minority ethnic group with extensive commercial and trading links in the region. Cathy Boone's observation echoes this situation. According to her, if ethnic politics enters the equation, it is often introduced by the elites as a strategy to manipulate identity in order to facilitate their rule.[16] In the case of Liberia, Doe was obliged to extend his network to other groups by appointments into the government and to seek loyalties from influential figures, such as Alhaji Gassimu Kromah. The exploitation of ethnic allegiances, the politicization of ethnic loyalties, became one of the most enduring characteristics of Liberian politics; they cannot, however, replace a state when it comes to representing the interests of the whole population. Only an independent state, rising above the mêlée, can address these cleavages, but certainly not a cocktail of different interests groups with only minimal links to the society as a whole. None of the functional characteristics that define a state was working in Liberia and this constituted the principal cause of the conflict.

THE CONSEQUENCE OF MALGOVERNANCE: CITIZENS IN REBELLION

When national institutions do not adequately address the problem of the society, one of the options available to citizens is rebellion. Charles Taylor was therefore able to tap into a largely disenfranchised national and exiled population to build a strong network of forces in his campaign to challenge and replace Doe. Some Liberians adhered to such discourse since they were dissatisfied with Doe and wanted him removed. State dysfunction, to restate the central argument, is the most important 'variable' to understand the profound reasons and the main causes of these wars. Other factors, such as environmental decay and cultural identity, may have had their importance, but state ineffectiveness, manifested in the form of the incapacity to incorporate critical masses of the population into a political structure is by far the central issue.

When a regime cannot deliver the most basic services to its citizens, such as public goods, when ministries are inefficient and clientelistic, when institutions are gangrened by rampant corruption, citizens abandon the public sector and become lethargic toward their civic duties. Because sovereign control and supervision of resources are not guaranteed, the citizens view the state as a comprador bourgeoisie and there is no sense of belonging to the same nation. In an evocative passage, Chinese philosopher Lin Yutang provides an insight of what happens in the absence of a state:

In a society where legal protection is not given to personal rights, indifference is always safe and has an attractive edge to it . . . Indifference is not a natural characteristic of the people, but a social attitude made necessary by the absence of legal protection . . . The survival value of indifference consists, therefore, in the fact that in the absence of protection of personal rights for 'humankind' it is difficult for them to take much interest in public affairs.[17]

There is no governmental legitimacy without accountability. Participation is non-existent and masses become isolated and are inclined to develop from the bottom strategies of survival as a result of the collapse of the regime that has failed in establishing linkages and pacts between the state and the society that it is supposed to govern. Sierra Leonean sociologist Ibrahim Abdullah has observed how the progressive impoverishment of segments of populations and a situation of despair had forced youths to develop strategies of survival. Uneducated and lacking the basic democratic culture, they shift away from seeking to join the elite and form a common cause and culture intended to change the system.[18] Such groups organize along ethnic or other fragmentary ties, but unite around a rationale for violent action to destroy the system in the corrupt and degenerate form that it has assumed responsibilities.[19]

Because the vulnerability of these states is a direct result of their internal fragility, they cannot, as we have seen, rely on coercion to ensure compliance. According to Olivier Hurley, warlords and militias can only exist in states in which structure, authority, power, law and civil order have fragmented.[20] Severe internal crises are the result of the inadequacy of state structures and if ethnicity matters, this is because it is often introduced and manipulated by leaders as a political force. State weaknesses, exclusion, socio-economic frustrations and institutional fragility are the most important causes. These pathologies were manifest in the Liberian crisis. Therefore, efforts to 'bring the state back in' are paramount to addressing the root causes of these conflicts. The building or reordering of these states is fundamentally the initial step. A region is not an abstract concept. Nor does it operate in a vacuum. It is a reality, based on cooperation between states on issues and priorities they have identified. A region is composed of states and if these political entities sink in disorder, not only will the concept of regional development fail to emerge, but the region itself will be in danger of instability due to the spill-over effects of the conflicts on neighboring countries as illustrated in Liberia.

PROTECTING RIGHTS AND PROMOTING JUSTICE
THROUGH STATE LEGITIMACY

One may confidently argue that the Liberian crisis has its origins in the absence of a functioning state. When Liberia experienced its first civilian regime following the 1985 elections, the first nine months of Doe's administration were described in the following terms:

> Nine turbulent months later, President Doe was still groping for a degree of legitimacy, which he had hoped—and miserably failed—to gain in the October 1985 election. His government was reeling from crisis to crisis, alternately releasing political detainees and then jailing new ones, repealing military decrees and then clamping down on dissent, lifting a ban on one newspaper and shutting down another.[21]

Intellectuals and experienced civil servants who lacked political or socio-ethnic connections were isolated by the Doe regime. As one specialist of Liberian politics notes:

> Those tapped to administer the government at the administrative level were mainly a pool of less sophisticated professionals or mere opportunists seeking a part in an event, which had disintegrated into a financially rewarding political satire. Therefore, they lacked the adequate facility to devise policy and related mechanisms to ameliorate the deteriorating conditions. As a direct result, each sought to hex up vile designs to sustain a place in Doe's preferred circle, often to the detriment of their (those whom they considered as competitors) peers.[22]

The lack of expertise and adequate human capital combined with limited economic resources strongly suggests that Liberia was not a functioning apparatus. Its civil servants were never able to achieve the goals set by incumbents to initiate reforms or to coherently organize state officials around goals set in an agenda. The state was concentrated in the hands of the "strongman" and his family and friends. Armed groups found in the legitimate demands of the vast majority of the population demagogic justifications to challenge the state. This pattern of political process is so familiar that African leaders are always heeding that threat.[23] In other words, conflict is so endemic in most of these *de facto* fragmenting states that military oppression of citizens remains one of the few resorts for these regimes to continue their existence. Liberia is such a revealing exemplar of this phenomenon as the weakening of the Doe regime pushed a number of them to identify with the malaise, thereby creating the need of a national survivor. Charles Taylor proclaimed himself to be that man. He publicly announced his intention to oust Doe and declared "the only good Doe is a dead Doe."[24]

Though the declared purpose of Taylor's invasion was to end a tyrannical regime, previous coverage has shown how fanatically he decided to be the president of Liberia, and how conflictual was his rise to power. Since then, his record has included a plethora of cruelties that are well known to occupy us here. Human rights observers, NGOs and international organizations have consistently charged his regime with crimes, including the execution of ministers and other prominent Liberian leaders such as Jackson F. Doe (no relative to Samuel Doe).[25] Once again, given how Taylor came to power, this is not surprising. Similar political problems are sweeping West Africa, and until resolved at the national level, the idea of a regional approach, no matter what its priorities are—conflict management or economic development—will remain in the realm of wishful thinking.

FUNCTIONING STATES AS A PREREQUISITE TO REGIONAL INTEGRATION

The vitality of a region depends on the states that form it. A region does not operate *ex nihilo*. Regional organizations constitute first and foremost activities by states in one or several issues areas. Andrew Hurrell refers to "a set of policies by one or more states designated to promote the emergence of a cohesive regional unit, which dominates the pattern of relations between the states of that region and the rest of the world, and which form the organizing basis for policy within the region across a range of issues."[26] At the present time, most West African states are unable to perform the quintessential basic tasks of maintaining law and order within their borders. As early as the eighties, they had been declared fragile,[27] 'juridicially sovereign but empirically non-functioning' 'a source for suffering and disorder.'[28]

For others, they are internally incoherent and externally manipulated. They are seen as 'underdeveloped,' 'overdeveloped,' 'fictive,' 'quasi' or 'pseudo' states. States are needed first, yet the state in Africa is dysfunctional, patrimonial, corrupt, fraudulent, 'rentier' and 'parasitic.' Each of these terms expresses a malaise and reflects the crises facing African states. Recent and popularized literature termed them "failed states" i.e. governments that are internationally recognized but face severe political crisis and are incapable of providing domestic conditions of peace, order and good government.[29] W. Zartman summarizes well their main characteristics:

> As the decision function of government, the state is paralyzed and inop-
> erative. Laws are not made, order is not preserved, and societal cohe-
> sion is not enhanced. As a territory, it is no longer assured security and
> provision by a central sovereign organization. As the authoritative
> political institution, it has lost its legitimacy. As a system of socio-eco-
> nomic organization, its functional balance of inputs and outputs is
> destroyed.[30]

State institutions function as a façade, disconnected from the sources of
real political power and detached from the society. The state does not perform on the basis of generally accepted principles of legitimacy or governmental institutions, but governmental activities are informal, arbitrary, and
characterized by various degrees of improvisation, lack of creativeness,
professionalism and talent. State authority is often an additional instrument or source of power which comfortably affords advantages to the
political leaders. Political leaders deliberately and consciously weaken institutions and undermine the state which becomes a threat to peace because
its excessive authoritarianism, abruptness and arbitrariness lead to serious
assaults from large numbers of groups such as rebels, militias, child soldiers, and unemployable youths who are among the driving forces behind
the new wars in West Africa. The region is filled with insurgent groups
whose only agenda is the overthrow of the incumbent regimes which refuse
to concede to majority rule.

All over West Africa, armed groups, supported by leaders in the sub-
region, are moving from one country to another. They do not have any constructive reforms; their only objective is directed towards a change of
leadership or, sometimes, towards the mere seizure of natural resources.
These wars are means for the accumulation of wealth. Warlords do not seek
the creation of a state different from the one they overthrow, nor do they
have a political agenda.[31] To what extent does Charles Taylor's conception
of a regime differ from that of Doe's? In Liberia, Sierra Leone and Côte
d'Ivoire, none of the factions that are challenging the existing states and
their leaders have spelled out political reasons for waging war. I am not stat-
ing that they did not refer to politics in their discourses: what I maintain is
that none of the armed groups have provided any coherent plan for fundamentally changing for example, Liberia's political and economic structures
and society. All defended their struggles in vague terms based more on a
personal desire to access to the presidency, deposit national resources in foreign banks than on a political project for the country. Taylor claimed to be
waging a war to remove Doe and to bring democracy but opposed the principle of democratic elections for several years. Factions and their leaders

have claimed to be fighting for democratic rights but their credentials are dubious because when they lack popular support, they impose their will on the population. Those cruelties are well known.

It is pretended that the new wars are difficult to understand. Banditry, piracy and a huge market of international trafficking are the main reasons of these wars. They operate easily because the state cannot ensure its basic functions: the state is, in fact, the problem. One of the most dramatic consequences of the activities of these groups is that they are central to African politics; they are the principal movers of events. They are no longer clandestine organizations, but they openly seek legitimation and support of the population by presenting a vaguely populist, anti-establishment discourse to generate sympathy from many people not otherwise inclined to support them, but with whom they share a frustration over the existing politico-economic system. Socio-economic frustration does not legitimize any particular insurgent organization *per se*. The existence of injustice legitimizes opposition, but not any form of opposition. Further, these groups refuse the mediation of African leaders as their objective is to become internationally recognized, but international legitimacy refers to other norms in terms of the transfer of sovereignty. In an exaggerated description of the region, Robert Kaplan notes:

> The withering away of central governments, the rise of tribal and regional domains . . . the growing pervasiveness of war in West Africa is reverting to the Africa of the Victorian Atlas. It consists now of a series of coastal trading posts, such as Freetown and Conakry, and an interior that, owing to violence, volatility and disease, is again becoming as Graham Greene once observed, "blank" and "unexplored."[32]

Kaplan's image of West Africa is racially prejudiced, because it is very similar to that of barbarism that was painted of the nineteenth century to justify colonization as the "white man's burden"; nevertheless some of its elements cannot be dismissed. The issue here is not whether anyone has a mission to seek desperate places and govern them. The fundamental question is how to prevent constant wars and barbarism. How are the continued violence, civil genocide, civilian cleansing, threat to the human existence of citizens, and the instability of neighbors to be prevented? Some of these states are at the stage of premodern politics. This assessment of the situation is not a sweeping generalization but, with all due caution, many West African states are not functioning ones. Liberia, Sierra Leone, Guinea, Côte d'Ivoire are not exceptions. Sénégalese authorities, despite public declarations, have not found yet any solutions to the Casamance insurrection, which is in constant danger of exploding. Burkina Faso's involvement in many of these conflicts presents a risk. Nowhere does order and social justice really exist, and to worsen the situation, irresponsible leaders are creating and supporting cross-border invasions that threaten regional peace and security and undermine agriculture-based entities. A recent UN panel of experts has recorded:

> It is frequently the case that political victories assume a 'winner-takes-all' form with respect to wealth and resources, patronage, and the prestige and prerogatives of office . . . Where there is insufficient accountability of leaders, lack of transparency in regimes, inadequate checks and balances, non adherence to the rule of law, absence of peaceful means to change or replace leadership, or lack of respect for human rights, political control becomes excessively important, and the stakes become dangerously high. This situation is exacerbated when, as is often the case in Africa, the State is the major provider of employment and political parties are largely as either regionally or ethnically based.[33]

This report is courageous and accurate. By focusing exclusively on the national origins of these problems, the UN is calling for efforts to overcome leadership weaknesses and intolerance, bureaucratic corruption and ineffectiveness. The role of the international community, already limited, may be further reduced as the following passage of the report implies:

> Within the context of the United Nations' primary responsibility for matters of international peace and security, providing support for regional and subregional initiatives in Africa is both necessary because the United Nations lacks the capacity, resources and expertise to address all problems that may arise in Africa. It is desirable because the international community should strive to complement rather that supplant African efforts to resolve Africa's problems.[34]

This assertion means that nobody is ready to take the role of supporting such an excessive burden. Therefore, it seems highly doubtful to explain the UN disengagement in West Africa by the measure of success that ECOMOG intervention achieved in Liberia.

It is highly debatable, as the report seems to suggest, that ECOWAS has much more experience than the United Nations on the issues of peace operations. Liberia was its first experience in humanitarian intervention. This discourse is mild in its tone but it is to be understood as a continuing disengagement from African affairs. The United Nations, even when it has resources, will no longer waste them on conflicts where the different actors are not committed to cooperate for peace. It needs to rationalize them and to make choices. And if rationality counts, support shall go to conflicts where actors are seeking peace, are committed to peace, and are seriously involved in finding a lasting solution. If the main players of a conflict are not committed to peace, there is nothing that the international community can achieve. Robert I. Rotberg aptly summarizes my general argument:

> These kleptocratic, patrimonial leaders . . . give Africa a bad name, plunge its people into poverty and despair, and incite civil wars and bitter internal conflict. They are the ones largely responsible for declining GDP levels, food scarcities, rising infant-mortality rates, soaring budget deficits, human rights abuses, breaches of the rule of law, and prolonged serfdom for millions even in Africa's nominal democracies.[35]

This is true in a multitude of cases. What then are the implications? They are two: military intervention is not a viable option in these conflicts, and the leadership problem needs to be resolved.

THE OBSTACLES OF FAILED LEADERSHIP

The blame for internal conflicts cannot be placed only on rebel groups, but because they originate in weak or illegitimate leadership, leaders must also assume blame. Leadership in Africa has regularly been decried by social scientists especially 'Afro-pessimists.'

One thesis is the 'criminalization of the state,' which argues that many African leaders are uninterested in any form of legitimacy and are simply plundering the resources of their countries and exploiting whatever illicit opportunities arise to enrich themselves.[36] A second thesis argues that legitimacy in African political systems derives from patronage, so that African states are marked by dispensing patrimony, the 'recycling' of elites, and the use of state resources for the consolidation of power through unproductive investment in social and political networks[37] Samuel Doe in Liberia forcefully took power and then used barbaric methods to retain it. Often African internal problems are the result of permissive conditions such as abuse of political power, mismanagement and the absence of resources redistribution. Management of resources is the key to leadership. African leaders manage the resources that are available; they rarely create new or additional resources. Is dropping bombs that kill civilians the solution? Is military intervention the solution? In many cases the opponents who have pretended to liberate their country have proved to be more repressive than their predecessors. Is Taylor more protective of human rights than Doe? We will never know the difference between Mobutu Sese Seko and Laurent Desire Kabila. It is rare in Africa today to find a head of state that acts on behalf of an entire nation. People are not governed and countries are candidates for state failure. Is the façade of armed humanitarism the solution to these problems?

These problems are political and so require political solutions that are largely in the hands of the elite and the citizens. Building viable states, politically organized and ordered, is the most urgent task in West Africa and humanitarian intervention cannot achieve this goal. The international community cannot build a nation. It can provide assistance, expertise, observers, ombudsdsmans, facilitators, and conciliators. The same can be said about democracy and the rule of law. Democracy does not grow suddenly because leaders have adopted another declaration or an additional protocol. The rule of law, at all levels, requires daily reciprocity and patriotism on the part of leaders and citizens. It remains to be seen if a government based on dubious manipulated political processes, known as brutal and lacking legitimacy, will respect the decisions of an African court of justice. The rule of law is not only a regional or international proclamation: it needs to be respected, sustained, and constantly maintained by the state. Most African legal documents are good on paper but *juris effectus in executione consistit.*

Somalia, Rwanda, The Democratic Republic of Congo, and Liberia have revealed both the incapacity and the lack of enthusiasm of the international community to involve itself in nation building. It cannot do it. It even failed to stop genocide and the terrible disaster in the Democratic Republic of Congo for many years. States are imploding and entering the lexicon of political collapse one after another. Statesmen and academics engaged in the political hope of regionalism should accept that African states are dysfunctional and address that problem before going further. Regionalism in Africa will have to start by the reconstruction of these states first; otherwise it will not happen if one talks about substance, not the signature of many treaties. These states, for most of them, are 'corrupt,' 'authoritarian,' 'prebendal,' 'patrimonial' 'sultanic,' 'kleptocratic,' 'predatory,' 'rentier,' 'praetorian,' even 'decertified.' These problems are not resolved because leaders meet in a summit and publicly adopt a mechanism that reaffirms the urgency of good governance and human rights. This is fallacious because if leaders are committed to good governance they need to apply it at home first. Good governance is not an article of faith. Good governance is not the signature of a treaty. Good governance is not about international meetings. It is not about ordinary or extraordinary summits. Poor governance is not resolved because a mechanism is adopted at the regional level. These laws need to be applied. Good governance is first and foremost a fundamentally national responsibility. We are reminded by James March and Johan Olsen that national institutions are the pillars of good governance. According to these authors, governance is organized around four major tasks:

- Developing identities of citizens and groups in the political environment creating and supporting civic institutions;

- Developing capabilities for appropriate political action among citizens, groups and institutions fulfilling the expectations of relevant rules, norms and duties;

- Developing accounts of political events defining the meaning of history, the options available, and the possibilities for action;

- Developing an adaptive political system coping with changing demands and environments that is making political learning and change possible.[38]

Good governance is an essential condition at the national level. It is first and foremost a commitment toward its own citizens by the state. It requires effectiveness of national bureaucracies, efficiency, accountability and transparent legitimacy at the national level. Good governance is not region-oriented but state-oriented. It is nothing more than changing the existing political practices of "bad governance" in African countries and this is fundamentally an internal matter. The World Bank has defined good governance as "the exercise of political power to manage a nation's affairs."[39] Stated differently, good governance is the rules that set the conduct of politics: "Governance is the conscious management of regime structures with a view to enhancing the legitimacy of the public realm. . . . Legitimacy is the dependent variable produced by effective governance."[40] Therefore, governance is conceived as the opposite of current practices and behavior of many of those who hold offices in Africa. By focusing only on the adoption of mechanisms, the current discourse on governance is a form of *trompe l'oeil,* an Orwellian 'double speak,' a source of economic rent, a game of make-believe with the only objective to request aid from Western donors and loans from lending agencies.

The challenge for African states is not to redefine the concept of sovereignty or to declare it obsolete, but to understand and accept its meaning in its domestic aspects. Advocates of humanitarian intervention argue that sovereignty means responsibility but that responsibility is not that of the international community. The ethics of state responsibility implies that the state authorities are responsible for the protection of the lives of citizens and the promotion of human rights. This requires government legitimacy and functioning states; otherwise African regional organizations will continue to lack independence from the global system and will continue to be a forum for annual summits with rhetoric, speeches, accolades, communiqués and declarations.

Conclusion

The problem in the West African crisis was not so much the obsolescence of the principles of international law, but that they were not observed. I have argued that the ECOWAS intervention was a poor example of justifying the obsolescence of the current norms of international society and an uncertain model for future armed interventions. The justifications, grounded on the principles of democracy and human rights, are at best problematic. Humanitarian considerations are not a legal basis for intervention. Undertaken by a group of military regimes and undemocratic states, it resembles a camouflage of other interests. These interests have been manifested in different forms. Nigeria's army supported Samuel Doe and the different factions opposed to Taylor who, on the other hand, received support from Côte d'Ivoire and Burkina Faso as well as from abroad.[1] Nigerian-led intervention in Liberia was a classic example of the appetite for power. The abuse of its dominant position illustrates that even when a neighboring country undertakes intervention under humanitarian claims it cannot be taken for granted that it is guided by the best of intentions. Political and other considerations always play a major role. The dilemma constitutive of the basic international legal principles and the power configuration behind humanitarian intervention are well emphasized in the following passage:

> International law and society are still caught propounding contradictory principles: on the one hand the sovereignty of states and non-intervention in their internal affairs, and on the other hand human rights; on the one hand the equality of states, and on the other the special privileges of the five permanent members of the UN Security Council . . . Power is still the key factor in international relations even if it is more ambiguous in its character, more varied in its forms, and less of an

over-arching goal which can be single-mindedly pursued without reference to other considerations, than some of the so-called 'realists'
implied.[2]

International law, to the contrary of what advocates of humanitarian intervention have argued, consists of the voluntarily accepted principles regulating state actions within the community of states.[3] It is first and foremost
intended to develop rules to guide the interactions among sovereign states.
As J. L. Brierly puts it, "international law may be defined as the body of
rules and principles of action which are binding upon civilized states in
their relations with one another."[4] Undeniably, all sovereign states do not
occupy the same position in international society but they enjoy a fundamental legal equality, that is, they are all subject to the same rules and to
the same duties. These rules protect states against the use of force in international affairs. In the Corfu Channel Case, the International Court of Justice argued that neither the United Nations nor its member states had an
inherent right of intervention against other states. Two fundamental, inter-
related assumptions of public international law justify this position. First
states are independent from any other authority and therefore have their
right to sovereignty in their territories. They do not need to respect human
rights or to be democratic in order to be recognized as legitimate. The second is a consequence of the first: because states are sovereign, they are also,
according to the law, assumed equal. Therefore, no state can dictate to
another state the *modus operandi* it should follow. In the domain of international human rights, treaties require states to observe well-defined standards and accepted principles, but they do not state that their violations
constitute a legal basis for military intervention.

A group of international lawyers and political leaders have argued that
humanitarian intervention is legal in certain circumstances. Bernard Kouchner the founder of Médecins sans Frontières challenged the importance of
sovereignty in a situation of human suffering.[5] Prime Minister Tony Blair
supported the legality of armed intervention to promote "values." He
declared that states were "mutually dependent" and that "our actions are
guided by a more subtle blend of mutual self interest and moral purpose in
defending the values we cherish."[6] In another intervention at the Labour
Party Conference, he called for a new international order to be obtained by
freedom and justice; "justice to bring those same values of democracy and
freedom to people around the world." To create the new world order that
Prime Minister Blair called for would entail putting the needs of underdeveloped countries before the interests of the international capitalist system. It is
doubtful that Western political leaders are ready to take that political risk.

Prime Minister Blair, who called for that new order, was not himself willing to sacrifice the interests of his companies as he publicly supported Western pharmaceutical companies in their determination to maintain high prices, unaffordable for pregnant, HIV positive women in South Africa or in developing countries.[7] At the time he delivered his speech, his government had approved the immensely controversial sale of a US $40 million military air traffic control system by British Aerospace to Tanzania, thereby compromising the poverty reduction programmes in health and education of one of the world's poorest countries.[8] There is a huge gap between prime ministerial public declarations and foreign policies realities. His paternalistic speeches and rhetoric, when confronted by his personal actions, confirmed the reality that altruism, as argued, is at the periphery of international affairs.

Similarly, moral attitudes are secondary to international law, which is based on the ethics of the state system. Legal precepts do not authorize intervention on humanitarian grounds or on the basis of lack of commitment to human rights. The only clear legal exceptions to the rule of non-intervention are the right to self-defense, whether, by an individual state or a collective regional security organization; and the collective measures authorized by the United Nations under Article 42 provided that peaceful means have failed. As discussed above, ECOWAS on that ground could have legitimately based its justifications under Article 4 of the 1981 ECOWAS Defense Protocol which empowers ECOWAS to initiate collective intervention in any internal armed conflict within any state, engineered and supported actively from outside likely to endanger the security and peace of the entire community. Article 6 (3) and Article 17 empower the Authority to decide on the expediency of military action, which validates both the creation of the SMC as well as a peacekeeping force between the warring factions and the subsequent political mediation. But this legal analysis weakens when one goes beyond pure legalism and examines the destabilizing role the same states played.

The anarchy created by the leaders and interveners, their unreasonable and unjust involvement confirm the relevance and the need to respect the juridical ethics of international law:

> Every ethical system must insist on the priority of its own legal principles,—or else it undermines its claim to be an ethical system- a system entitled to guide and govern human conduct. Legal systems, too, must insist on the priority of their own principles, or else they surrender their authority and become simply one, possibly indispensable, means for achieving ends that are defined by other ethical system. What holds true for law in general holds also for international law. As a normative

system, international law is concerned with whether or not particular acts or policies are lawful, not whether they are desirable or morally justifiable. For international law to provide a consistent and authoritative way of dealing with the question of lawfulness, the answers it generates must derive from its own traditions and procedures and not from the argument of moralists or philosophers.[9]

International law is not concerned with democratic credentials or popular sovereignty but looks at state sovereignty; and human rights violations are not *per se* a legal basis for armed intervention. West African states, or more generally African states, have always been within their rights when objecting to any attempts by developed states to intervene in their internal affairs. During the revival of the debate on humanitarian intervention, African states firmly contested the existence of the right to intervene and embraced the perspective adopted by the major powers of the developing world:

> Because each country has different national characteristics, there are varying perceptions and practices with regard to human rights . . . The main responsibility for protecting human rights rests with governments. The principle of non-interference in the internal affairs of other nations is applicable to the question of human rights . . . The importance of the relationship between collective human rights and world peace and development must be emphasized.[10]

African states on many occasions have expressed the same suspicion and have feared that the recognition of interference will serve the interest and the will of the most powerful states at the cost of the weak. At the general level of discussion on intervention, respect for the rule of law is in the interest of African countries as it is the only way they can deal equally with the big states. The rule of non-intervention must be reaffirmed and the empirical evidence presented here supports the argument that the Liberian crisis did not justify moving beyond non-intervention.

What was the main problem in the sub-region? As documented, member states of ECOWAS tolerated, organized, assisted, and financed subversive armed activities directed towards the regime of other state. These acts are expressly enumerated and prohibited by the International Court of Justice and the General Assembly.[11] Respecting these dispositions would have helped in dealing with the crisis. It is therefore, wrong to justify the intervention in Liberia by invoking the need for evolving norms especially by pointing out to the obsolescence of non-intervention and state sovereignty. Irresponsibility and a lucrative business were among the most important problems. According to one author ECOMOG became involved in illicit activities and concentrated "on stripping the country of fixed assets—railroad stock, mining equipment, and public utilities—and selling them abroad." He further notes that the Liberian Peace Council (LPC), a rival group of Taylor, used his Nigerian backers and ECOMOG soldiers to operate a rubber plantation firm that exported about 3,000 tons of rubber through Buchanan in 1994, netting an estimated $1.5 million.[12] These are the resources that have helped fuel the war and have made disarmament impossible. This is not humanitarian intervention, which is rooted in our obligation as human beings—individuals and in our societies—to allow and help one another to flourish as human beings.[13] The practice of humanitarian intervention has always revealed something else.

For more than a decade, UN Security Council resolutions, reports of special missions, independent experts, NGO reports and ECOWAS officials have condemned the destabilizing role of member states in the sub-regional crisis:

> It is appalling that Guinea—a current member of the Security Council-has flouted the arms embargo in Liberia. . . . The Guinea-backed rebel groups, Liberian United for Reconciliation and Democracy (LURD), fought forces loyal to Liberian President Charles Taylor . . . Guinea's Ministry of Defense ordered mortars and other ammunitions from Iran and arranged their onward transport to LURD.[14]

In situation after situation, armed groups in the region continued to benefit from support by allies in the region. The main armed movement in Liberia, the Movement for Democracy in Liberia, drew on support from Côte d'Ivoire. It has been documented that the Côte d'Ivoire government recruited fighters for its own conflict with the promise that they could "keep arms and take them back to Liberia."[15] The lack of impartiality and the disorder created by these states triumphed over successful mediation. ECOWAS sponsored a series of peace agreements, starting in November 1990 with the Bamako Agreement to address the underlying issues of the civil war. West African diplomatic initiatives, as the narrative summary provided here has shown, were ineffective and resulted in repeated failures. They were unable to mediate efficiently between the initial warring factions (NPFL, INPFL and AFL) which later fragmented, rendering the search of solution much more complex. It is when the UN and outsiders got involved that diplomacy made more progress. The very commitment of ECOWAS states to greater security was and still is in question. ECOWAS operates under anarchy; it is not yet a coherent sub-regional organization. There are great discussions on the role of ECOWAS, rhetoric, discourse, regular meetings, signature of new mechanisms, adoption of treaties; the organization however, lacks effective political processes. Serious legal instruments and constitutions, credible regional or national projects, should be free of any kind of demagogy, inapplicable provisions, or proclamations to embellish the façade. ECOWAS is a forum of announcement and ratifications, but concrete achievements are delayed dreams. There is nothing to celebrate. On the contrary, it is the United Nations' responsibility to acknowledge that, at the present time, ECOWAS cannot police the sub-region. Based on its experience with ECOMOG in Liberia, the international organization is well aware that without its technical and political support, and the involvement of its specialized UN agencies, the "pioneering mission" of ECOWAS in Liberia could not have had a chance of success.[16]

The truth is that stability never was achieved in Liberia fifteen years after the start of the war. The idea of regional responsibility is a West African myth due to the absence of political will and unity, the lack of military capabilities, the scarcity of resources, and, behind that myth, is concealed a disengagement of the UN from protracted African conflicts. The most compelling and urgent task for the West African states is the problem of fragmenting, failing, and chaotic states entities. There is no situation where armed intervention could provide a solution to these problems. West African states need to commit to the norms and rules of international relations in their relations and dealings with one another. The highest priority is to build functioning and legitimate states that are the only way to address the root causes of these conflicts. There is no alternative to that. One of the major obstacles to the emergence of a democratic society and to political development is that national leaders operate under discretionary and arbitrary rules. Without functioning states regional integration is a mere proposal. The intervention in Liberia and ECOWAS diplomacy into the conflict has led to chaos, confusion and disorder. To a large extent, the regional level has been a duplication of what is being done by national governments. These governments have not yet provided a model of performance. To transfer their functioning rules to the regional level does not strengthen good governance but rather makes it worse.

The community adopted a treaty on democracy and good governance in Dakar, Sénégal, in 2001. It declared as constitutional principles shared by all member states the separation of powers, the strengthening of parliaments, and the independence of the judiciary. It recognized that the rule of law involves a good judicial system and the promotion of human rights are essential factors for development. There is nothing new in these declarations. National constitutions already have dispositions on governance and political participation but they are not rigorously respected and leaders operate under capricious rules. Leaders need to go beyond rhetoric and promulgation and undertake concrete actions to provide for the basic needs of their populations. General living standards have drastically dropped, health, education, welfare, and housing expenditures have declined, life expectancy has declined, states are dangerous and countries suffer instability and violence. In fact, governance means only a government's capacity to manage social and economic resources to attain development. Quite often, poor governance is the result of the weakening of national institutions. Montesquieu observed that "at birth of new polities, leaders mold institutions, whereas afterwards institutions mold leaders."[17] This is not the case in many West African regimes where institutions are clientelistic. The state apparatus is dominated by the party in power, which, in most cases, is the majority party. The widespread lack of political participation is not only a central social problem but it also undermines African public discourses on good governance. West African leaders ignore the functional separation of state and party; they fail to distinguish between their mission as statesmen and those of members of the political parties to which they belong. This brings us to the problem of confusion of powers and its effects on governance.

The effectiveness of good governance is to be judged on its day-to-day execution. It is not good governance when the judiciary is usurped or when the executive often interferes in the decision making-process, because neutrality is not guaranteed. Impartiality, transparency and accountability constitute the *noyau dur* of judicial independence. They are fundamental for the protection of liberties and human rights. Without the independence of the judiciary, the effective protection of constitutional rights cannot be achieved, not certainly by a remote regional court. Commitment to human rights and good governance starts at home by respecting the decisions of national judges, supporting their independence, securing fair and transparent appointments, promotions and disciplinary actions. There is a lot to do in all these West African countries.

The separation of powers as an indicator of good governance posits also that the legislative branch should not be the instrument of the head of state. It must be a counterweight, not a creature of the executive. National assemblies are not critical fora of debate on vital issues. The most important decisions are made with very little consultation and institutional participation of parliaments. Assemblies lack the capacity, the organization, equipment and the experienced staff to serve as a mature and autonomous point of deliberation in the policy process. They are often "talking shops" places for the glorification of the head of state who in fact, has the real authority. Rules, institutions and written constitutions exist, and they are good, but the president dominates the state apparatus. Robin Theobold notes that "some of the new states are not states at all; rather they are virtually the private instruments of those powerful enough to rule."[18] While the constitutions give members of parliaments legislative oversight and budgetary powers, they are exercised to a limited extent, if at all. As former Sénégalese Prime Minister Dia has noted:

> African legislatures all too often lack much of the critical information essential to the exercise of legislative oversight. Typically opposition parties speak generally for the disaffected and impecunious intelligentsia and masses. The wealthy entrepreneurs are generally either non-nationals or in connivance with the ruling party and its government.[19]

Nicolas van de Walle aptly comments that "power was personalized because it was never properly institutionalized."[20] If these problems and dysfunctions are not resolved, the gap between announcement and realization will remain. There is certainly nothing to oppose the intention of West African states to cooperate, coordinate and harmonize their common goals. It remains to be seen how it would be possible without national institutions capable of effective decision taking and implementation. In short, states are the carriers of the regional ideal.

Notes

NOTES TO THE INTRODUCTION

1. Hedley Bull, *Intervention in World Politics* (Oxford: Clarendon Press, 1984), p. 181.
2. Stanley Hoffmann, "The problem of Intervention," in Hedley Bull, *Intervention in World Politics*, p. 7.
3. James Rosenau, "Intervention as a Scientific Concept," *Journal of Conflict Resolution*, (1969), p. 149.
4. Hedley Bull, *Intervention in World Politics*, pp. 193–195.
5. Robert O. Keohane, "Introduction," in Robert O. Keohane and J. L. Holzgrefe, (eds.), *Humanitarian Intervention: Ethical, Legal and Political Dilemmas* (Cambridge: Cambridge University Press, 2003), p. 1.
6. Emmerick de Vattel, *Le Droit des Gens ou Principe de la Loi Naturelle* (London: 1758).
7. R. J. Vincent, *Nonintervention and International Order* (New Jersey: Princeton University Press, 1974), p. 13.
8. Olivier Ramsbotham and Tom Woodhouse, *Humanitarian Intervention* (Cambridge, Mass: Blackwell Publishers Ltd, 1996), p. 3; Robert Jackson, *The Global Covenant: Human Conduct in a World of States* (Oxford and New York: Oxford University Press, 2000), p. 250.
9. Sean D. Murphy, *Humanitarian Intervention: The United Nations in an Evolving World Order* (Philadelphia: University of Pennsylvania Press, 1996), pp. 11–12.
10. J. L. Holzgrefe, "The Humanitarian Intervention Debate," in J. L. Holzgrefe and Robert O. Keohane (eds.), *Humanitarian Intervention* (Cambridge: Cambridge University Press, 2003), p. 18.
11. Fernando R. Tesòn, *A Philosophy of International Law* (Boulder: Westview Press, 1998); Joseph A. Camilleri and Jim Falk, The End of Sovereignty?: The Politics of a Shrinking and Fragmenting World (Brookfield, VT: Ashgate Publishing Company, 1992), p. 2; Simon Caney, "Humanitarian Intervention and State Sovereignty," in Andrew Walls (ed.), *Ethics and International Affairs* (Oxford: Rowman&Littlefield, 2000), pp. 117, 120–121; Michael

Smith, "Humanitarian Intervention: An Overview of the Ethical Issues," *Ethics and International Affairs* 12 (1998), pp. 64–79

12. W. Michael Reisman, "Humanitarian Intervention to protect the Ibos," in R. Lillich (ed.), *Humanitarian Intervention and the United Nations* (Charlottesville, VA: University of Virginia Press, 1973), p. 173.

13. Louis B. Song, "The New International Law: Protection of the Rights of Individuals rather Than of States," *American Journal of International Law Review* (1982), p. 7.

14. Danish Report, *Humanitarian Intervention Legal and Political aspects* (Copenhagen: Danish Institute of International Affairs, 1999).

15. W. Michael Reisman, "Sovereignty and Human Rights in Contemporary International Law," *American Journal of International Law* 84, (1990); Lawrence T. Farley, *Plebiscites and Sovereignty: The Crisis of Political Illegitimacy* (Boulder: Westview Press, 1986), p. 145.

16. Nicholas Onuf, "Sovereignty: Outline of a Conceptual History," *Alternatives* 16 (1991), p. 430.

17. Anthony D'Amato, "The invasion of Panama was a lawful Response to Tyranny," *American Journal of International Law*, 84 (1990), p. 874.

18. Fernando Tesòn, *Humanitarian Intervention: An Inquiry into Law and Morality* (2nd ed; NY: Transnational Publishers, 1997), pp. 55–61.

19. Tesòn, "The Ethics of Humanitarian Intervention," in R. L. Philips and D. L. Cady (eds.), *Humanitarian Intervention: Just War vs. Pacifism* (London: Rowman&Littlefield, 1996), pp. 1–6; see also Kofi Annan's speech to the UN General Assembly on 20 September 1999, "Two Concepts of Sovereignty," UN Press Release SG/SM/7136 GA/9596 of 20 September 1999.

20. Brian D. Lepard, *Rethinking Humanitarian Intervention: a fresh legal approach based on fundamental ethical principles in international law and world religions* (Pennsylvania: Pennsylvania State University Press, 2002), 1–36.

21. Nicholas J. Wheeler, *Saving Strangers* (Oxford and New York: Oxford University Press, 2000), p. 12; Jarat Chopra,"The New Subjects of International Law," Brown Foreign Affairs Journal (Spring 1991), pp. 27–30.

22. Richard Falk, *Revitalizing International Law* (Ames, Iowa: Iowa State University Press, 1989), p. 10.

23. The author emphasizes the point that popular sovereignty should not be the single variable that determines the lawfulness of intervention. See Michael Riesman, p. 874.

24. David J. Scheffer, "Toward a Modern Doctrine of Humanitarian Intervention," *University of Toledo Law Review*, 23, (Winter 1992), p. 259.

25. Judith Shklar, *Legalism* (Cambridge, Massachusetts: Harvard University Press, 1964), p. 106.

26. Myres McDougal, Michael Reisman, "Humanitarian Intervention to protect the Ibos," in Lillich (ed.), *Humanitarian Intervention*, p. 173.

27. Danish Report, p. 52.

28. "Convention on the Prevention and Punishment of the Crime of Genocide, 9 December 1948," Art VIII. For a critical view of the provisions, see L.

Kuper, *Genocide: Its Use in the Twentieth Century* (New Haven: Yale University Press 1982), pp. 36–39 and 174–185.

29. Barcelona Traction Case, ICJ Reports 1970, para.33–34.

30. Article 2 states: "In the present Convention, genocide means any of the following acts committed with intent to destroy, in whole or in part, a national, ethnical, racial or religious group, as such: a) killing members of the group; b) causing serious bodily or mental harm to members of the group; c) imposing measures intended to prevent births within the group; e) forcibly transferring children of the group to another group."

31. Secretary General Kofi Annan, Ditchley Lecture, June 26, 1998, p. 2.

32. Independent Commission on International Humanitarian Issues, *Modern Wars: The Humanitarian Challenge*. Quoted in Haas, 'Beware the Slippery Slope: Notes Toward the Definition of Justifiable Intervention' in Reed & Kaysen (eds.), *Emerging Norms of Justified Intervention* (Cambridge, Mass: American Academy of Arts and sciences, 1993), p. 164.

33. Michael Akehurst, "Humanitarian Intervention," in *Intervention in World Politics*, in Hedley Bull (ed.), p. 105; Peter Malanczuk, *Humanitarian Intervention and the Legitimacy of the Use of Force* (Inaugural Lecture University of Amsterdam, Amsterdam, 1994).

34. Carlos Calvo, *Le droit international et pratique; précédé d'un exposé historique des progrès de la science du droit des gens*, 5th edn. (Paris: A. Rousseau, 1896).

35. In several declarations such as the: 'Declaration on the Inadmissibility of Intervention in the Domestic Affairs of Sates' (1965), the 'Declaration on Principles of International Law on Friendly Relations and Cooperation among States in Accordance with the Charter of the United Nations (1970), the 'Declaration on the Inadmissibility of Intervention and Interference in the Internal Affairs of State' (1981) and the 'Declaration of the Enhancement of the Effectiveness of Non-Use of International Relations (1987), the General Assembly had prohibited to "intervene . . . for any reason whatsoever, in the internal or external affairs of any other state. Consequently, armed intervention and all other forms of interference or attempted threats against the personality of the state or against its political, economic and cultural element are in violation of international law."

36. *Nicaragua (Merits)*, [1986] ICJ Rep 14, 133 para. 263.

37. For an excellent survey of the principle see R. J. Vincent, *Human Rights and International Relations* (Cambridge; New York: Cambridge University Press, 1986).

38. T. Pakenham, *The Scramble for Africa 1876–1912* (London: Weidenfeld &Nicolson 1991) p. 22; A. Hochschild, *King Leopold's Ghost: A Story of Greed, Terror, and Heroism in Colonial Africa* (Boston: Houghton Mifflin, 1998), pp. 43–46.

39. Hedley Bull, *Intervention in World Politics*, p. 5.

40. Hans Morgenthau, *Politics Among Nations*, 2nd ed. (New York: Alfred A. Knopf, 1954), p. 48.

41. George F. Kennan, "Morality and Foreign Policy," *Foreign Affairs* 64 (Winter 1985–1986), p. 206; and *Realities of American Foreign Policy* (Princeton: Princeton University Press, 1954), p. 48.

42. Quoted in Noam Chomsky, *A New Generation Draws the Line: Kosovo, East Timor and the Standards of the West* (London and New York: Verso, 2000), p. 135.

43. J. C. Rufin, *Le piège humanitaire* (Paris: Claude Lattés, 1986).

44. See among others, Jerome Slater and Terry Nardin, "Non-Intervention and Human Rights," *Journal of* Politics, 48 (1986), p. 94; Michael Mandelbaum, "The Reluctance to Intervene," *Foreign Policy,* 95 (1995), p. 12.

45. Stanley Hoffman, *The Politics and Ethics of intervention;* Michael Bazyler "Reexamining the Doctrine of Humanitarian Intervention in Light of the Atrocities in Kampuchea and Ethiopia," *Stanford Journal of International Law,* 23 (1987), p. 547.

46. R. J. Vincent, *Human Rights and International Relations,* pp. 150–152.

47. J. Gus Liebenow, *Liberia: The Evolution of Privilege* (Ithaca, NY.: Cornell University Press, 1969); and by the same author, *Liberia: The Quest for Democracy* (Bloomington: Indiana University Press, 1987); Christopher Clapham, *Liberia and Sierra Leone: An Essay in Comparative Politics* (Cambridge: Cambridge University Press, 1976); Stephen Ellis, "Liberia 1989–1994: A Study of Ethnic and Spiritual Violence," *African Affairs* 94 (1995), pp. 165–197.

48. An early distinction was made between the settlers and the 'natives,' (the indigenous people). See Harold Nelson, "Historical Setting," in Harold Nelson, (ed.), *Liberia: A Country Study* (Washington, D.C.: American University, 1984), p. 22.

49. *Amnesty International* has recorded a catalogue of human rights violations between 1985 and 1989. See, among other publications, *Amnesty International Report* (1985) pp. 59–61; *Amnesty International Report* (1987) pp. 66–68 and *Amnesty International Report,* (1989) pp. 62–64.

50. *West Africa Magazine,* January 8–14, 1990.

51. *West Africa Magazine,* June 14–20, 1993.

52. For an examination of the major actors in the Liberian conflict as well as the external players, see George Klay Kieh, Jr., "Combatants, Patrons, Pacemakers, and the Liberian Conflict," *Studies in Conflict and Terrorism,* Vol. 15 (1992), pp. 125–143; William Reno "The Business of War in Liberia," *Current History* 95 (1996), p. 214.

53. David Wippman, "Enforcing the Peace: ECOWAS and the Liberian Civil War," in Lori Fisler Damrosch (ed.), *Enforcing Restraint: Collective Intervention in Internal Conflicts* (New York: Council on Foreign Relations Press, 1993), p. 165.

54. Mauritania withdrew its membership in 2000.

55. ECOWAS Standing Mediation Committee, Banjul, Republic of Gambia, Final Communiqué of the First Session, 7 August 1990; text in Mark Weller, (ed.), *Regional Peace-Keeping and International Enforcement: The Liberian crisis,* (Cambridge: Cambridge University Press, 1994), p. 73.

56. *West Africa Magazine*, Nov 26-Dec 2, 1990.
57. Herbert Howe, "Lessons of Liberia: ECOMOG and Regional Peacekeeping," *International Security*, Vol. 21/3 (1996/1997), p. 151.
58. UN Doc. S/RES/788 (1992).
59. Fernando R. Tesòn, "The liberal case for humanitarian intervention," in J. L. Holzgrefe and Robert O. Keohane (eds.), *Humanitarian Intervention,* op. cit., p. 93.
60. F. H. Hinsley, *Sovereignty* (New York: Basic Books, 1966).
61. Alan James, *Sovereign Statehood: The Basis of International Society* (London: Allen and Unwin, 1986).
62. Hinsley, *Sovereignty*, p. 1.
63. Robert Jackson, *The Global Covenant*, p. 156.
64. In civil and international law it is the principle that all agreements are concluded with the implied condition that they are binding only as long as there are no major changes in circumstances.
65. Thomas G. Weiss & Leon Gordenker (eds.), *NGOs, The UN, & Global Governance* (Boulder; London: Lynne Rienner Publishers, 1996); Laurie S. Wiseberg, "Human rights non-governmental organizations," in Richard Pierre Claude & Burns H. Weston (eds.), *Human rights in the World Community: issues and action* (Philadelphia: University of Pennsylvania Press: 1992), pp. 372–382.
66. Ralph Folsom, *European Union Law* (St Paul: West Group, 1999) pp. 65–75; Ian Brownlie, *Principles of Public International Law*, Fifth Edition, (Oxford: Clarendon Press, 1998) pp. 590–598; Joel Rideau, *Le Droit Des Communautés Européennes* (Paris: Presses Universitaires De France, 1995).
67. Murphy, S. D., *Humanitarian Intervention*, pp. 14–15.
68. Max Ahmadu Sesay, "Collective Security or Collective Disaster?" *Security Dialogue*, vol. 26 (2), 1995, p. 213.
69. Clement E. Adibe, "Coercive Diplomacy and the Third World: Africa After the Cold War." Paper presented to the Workshop on Coercive Diplomacy, King's College, London, 7-9 June 1995, p. 14.
70. Barry Buzan, *People, States, and Fear: An Agenda for International Security Studies in the Post-Cold War Era* (Boulder: Lynne Rienner, 1991).
71. ECOMOG Sold Weapons to Rebels. *The Independent*: Accra, January 20, 1999.
72. *Newsweek*, "Witness to Insanity," 29 April, 1996.
73. For a presentation of these advantages, see Boutros Boutros-Ghali, *An Agenda For Peace* (New York: United Nations, 1992) and Gareth Evans *Cooperating For Peace* (Canberra: Allen and Unwin, 1994).
74. Alex Okunnor, "Africa's Shining Example," *West Africa,* 24–30 March 1997.
75. Robert Jackson, *The Global Covenant: Human Conduct in a World of States* (Oxford and New York: Oxford University Press, 2000).
76. Aboagye, Festus B. *ECOMOG: a sub-regional experience in conflict resolution, management and peacekeeping in Liberia* (Accra: SEDCO, 1999);

Nass, I. A., *A Study in Internal Conflicts: The Liberian Crisis and the West African Peace Initiative* (Enugu, Nigeria: Fourth Dimensions Publishers, 2000).

77. Stephen Ellis, *The Mask of Anarchy: The destruction of Liberia and the Religious Dimension of an African Civil War* (New York: New York University Press, 1999).

78. Klaas Van Walraven, *The Pretence of Peace-keeping: ECOMOG, West Africa, and Liberia, 1990–1998* (The Hague: Netherlands Institute of International Relations, 1999); Karl Magyar and Earl Conteh-Morgan (eds.), *Peacekeeping in Africa: ECOMOG in Liberia* (London and New York: St. Martin's Press, 1998); M. A. Vogt, *The Liberian Crisis and ECOMOG: A Bold Attempt at Regional Peacekeeping* (Lagos: Gabumo, 1992); Olivier Furley, Roy May, (eds), *Peacekeeping in Africa* (Brookfield, Vt.: Ashgate, 1998).

79. Adekeye Adebajo, *Building Peace in West Africa: Liberia, Sierra Leone, and Guinea* (Boulder and London: Lynne Rienner Publishers, 2002); Adekeye Adebajo, Ismail Rashid (eds.), *West Africa's Security Challenges* (Boulder and London: Lynne Rienner Publishers, 2004).

80. Joseph E. Stiglitz, *Globalization and its discontents* (New York : Norton, 2002), p. iii.

81. Tesòn, *Humanitarian Intervention*, p. 76.

NOTES TO CHAPTER ONE

1. ECOWAS, Standing Mediation Committee, Decision A/DEC.1/8/90, on the Cease-fire and Establishment of an ECOWAS cease-fire Monitoring Group for Liberia, Banjul, Republic of Gambia, 7 August 1990.
2. See *Charter of the United Nations*, Article 2 (1).
3. Michael Walzer, among others, argues that the prohibition of military intervention is a key component of the legalist paradigm. See Michael Walzer, *Just and Unjust Wars: A Moral Argument with Historical Illustrations* (New York: Basics Books, 1977).
4. Sean D. Murphy, *Humanitarian Intervention*, p. 2. Similarly Robert Jackson argues that the Charter proclaims human rights but it does not include human rights as a specific ground for international intervention in state sovereignty. *The Global Covenant*, p. 253.
5. For different interpretations of art 2 (4) as a legal basis for humanitarian intervention: Richard B. Lillich, "Humanitarian Intervention: A Reply to Dr. Brownlie and a Plea for Constructive Alternatives," in *Law and Civil War in the Modern World*, John Norton Moore (eds.), pp. 229, 241, 251; J. P. Fonteyne, "The Customary International Law Doctrine of Humanitarian Intervention: Its Current Validity Under the UN Charter," *California Western International Law Journal* 4 (1974), p. 258; F. Tesòn, *Humanitarian Intervention*; J. Bierly, *The law of Nations*, (5th ed. 1955) pp. 309–310; H. Kelsen, *Principles of International Law* 2nd ed. 1968, p. 58; M. Akehurst, *A Modern Introduction to International Law*, 1984, pp. 219–21.

6. The use of force under Chapter VIII will be examined in subsequent chapters.

7. Walzer, *Just and Unjust Wars,* p. 62.

8. "Declaration on the Principles of International Law concerning Friendly Relations and Cooperation among States in accordance with the Charter of the United Nations," annexed to GA Res. 2625 of October 24, 1970 without a vote.

9. C. Gray, "The Principle of Non-Use of Force," in V. Lowe and C. Warbrick, (eds.), *The United Nations and the Principles of International Law* (London: Routledge, 1994), p. 34 ; Peter Malanczuk, *Humanitarian Intervention and the Legitimacy of the Use of Force,* p. 14.

10. [1949] ICJ Report 4.

11. In this case Article 2 (4) was regarded as a codification of customary international law. See *Case of Military and Paramilitary Activities in and Against Nicaragua* (Nicaragua v. United States of America), Merits, Judgment of June 27, 1986.

12. Gordon A. Christenson, "The World Court and Jus Cogens," *AJIL* 81 (1987) p. 93.

13. 1949 I.C.J. at 35.

14. This decision was adopted by twelve votes to three. It reads in part: "The United States of America, by certain attacks on Nicaraguan territory in 1983–1984. . . . and further by those acts of intervention referred to in subparagraph (3) hereof which involve the use of force, has acted, against the Republic of Nicaragua, in breach of its obligation under customary international law not to use force against another state, not to intervene in its affairs, not to violate its sovereignty. . . ."

15. Commentary of Article 50 of the International Law Commission. See I.L.C. *Yearbook,* 1966 (II) p. 247.

16. Ibid.

17. Protocol Relating to Mutual Assistance on Defense, arts 4, 16, 17 18.

18. Declaration on the Principles of International Law concerning Friendly Relations and Cooperation among States in Accordance with the Charter of the United Nations of 24 October 1970.

19. Michael Reisman, "Sovereignty and Human Rights in Contemporary International Law," *AJIL* 84 (1990), p. 866.

20. Simon Chesterman "Law, Subject and Subjectivity in International Relations: International Law and the Postcolony," *Melbourne University Law Review,* 20 (1996), p. 979; Reisman, "Sovereignty and Human Rights in Contemporary International Law," p. 874.

21. Reisman, p. 872.

22. J. G. Starke, "Human Rights and International Law," in Eugene Kamenka (ed.), *Human Rights* (London: Temple Smith, 1985), p. 7.

23. Michael J. Glennon, "The New Interventionism: The Search for a Just International Law," *Foreign Affairs* 78 (1999), pp 3–6.

24. See F. Tesòn, "The liberal case for humanitarian intervention," in Keohane and Holzgrefe (eds.), *Humanitarian Intervention,* p. 94.

25. Nicholas J. Wheeler, *Saving Strangers,* p. 11.

26. Statement by the U.S Secretary of State Madeleine Albright on the Release of the 1999 Human Rights Report, 25 February 2000.
27. R. J. Vincent, *Human Rights and International Relations*, p. 137.
28. Ibid.,
29. Vincent, p. 140.
30. Javier Javier Pérez de Cuéllar, *Report of the Secretary General on the Work of the Organization* (NY: United Nations, 1991), pp. 11–12.
31. UN Press Release SG/SM 4560, Apr. 24, 1991.
32. Quoted in Genes M. Lyons and Michael Mastanduno (eds.), *Beyond Westphalia* (Maryland: The John Hopkins University Press, 1995), p. 2.
33. Quoted in Sean D. Murphy, *Humanitarian Intervention*, p. 70.
34. International Commission on Intervention and State Sovereignty, *The Responsibility to Protect* (Ottawa: International Development Research Centre, 2001), p. 2.
35. Secretary General Nobel Lecture Press Release SG/SM 8071.
36. Article 2–3 of the Vienna Declaration and Programme of Action. Conf.157/23, 12 July 1993.
37. Seyom Brown, *Human Rights in World Politics* (New York: Longman, 2000), p. 74.
38. M. Ignatieff, *Human Rights as Politics and Idolatry* (Princeton: Princeton University Press, 2001), p. 35.

NOTES TO CHAPTER TWO

1. Adekeye Adebajo and Chris Landsbeg "The heirs of Nkrumah: Africa's New Investments," *Pugwash Series,* no 3.
2. Adekeye Adebajo and Chris Landsbeg, p. 3.
3. *West Africa Magazine,* Nov 26-Dec 2, 1990.
4. Ibid, 1990.
5. Salim A. Salim, "Africa's destiny," *West Africa* (1990) p. 2690.
6. Ibid, p. 2691.
7. Madagascar was not represented at the Durban summit in July 2002.
8. David Wippman, *Enforcing Restraint,* p. 179.
9. M. Weller, *Regional Peace-Keeping and International Enforcement: The Liberian Crisis* (Cambridge University Press, Cambridge: 1994), p. 39.
10. Letter of Doe to Chairman of ECOWAS. Reprinted in Weller, p. 40.
11. Martin Lowenkopf, "Liberia: Putting the State Back Together," in I. William Zartman (ed.), *Collapsed States: The Disintegration and Restoration of Legitimate Authority* (Boulder and London: Lynne Rienner Publishers, 1995), pp. 91–95.
12. *West Africa,* 1990, p. 2631.
13. The 1977 Geneva Protocols reaffirm the importance of humanitarian assistance for the victims of natural disasters and similar emergency situations.
14. On the existence of the right to humanitarian assistance with or without the consent of the state, see among others: Arthur C. Helton, "The Legality

of Providing Humanitarian Assistance Without the Consent of the Sovereign," *International Journal of Refugee Law,* 4 (1992), p. 375; Fritz Kalshoven, (ed.), *Assisting the Victims of Armed Conflicts and Other Disasters* (Dordrecht: Matinus Nijhoff Publishers, 1989).

15. Tesòn, *Humanitarian Intervention,* pp. 173–174.
16. Murphy, *Humanitarian Intervention,* p. 75.
17. Article 13 of the UN Charter.
18. S. D. Murphy, *Humanitarian Intervention,* p. 70
19. The I.C.J. noted that the preservation of human rights in Nicaragua could not justify the fact that the United States breached the customary principle of non use of force.
20. Ibid, 134.
21. United Nations Economic and Social Council, Commission on Human Rights (New York: United Nations, 1986), p. 3.
22. Adamantia Pollis and Peter Schwab (eds.), *Human Rights: Cultural and Ideological Perspectives* (New York: Praeger Publishers, 1979), p. xiii.
23. Jack Donnelly, *Universal Human Rights in Theory and Practice* (Ithaca: Cornell University Press, 1989), especially chapter 3.
24. For an approach to human rights within the North-South context including the debate on cultural relativism, see R. J. Vincent, *Human Rights and International Relations.*
25. Chapter XI of the United Nations Charter especially article 73.
26. Adam Roberts, "The So-Called Right of Humanitarian Intervention," *Yearbook of International Humanitarian Law,* Vol. 3 (2000), p. 33.
27. J. S. Mill, *On Liberty* (Indianapolis: Bobbs-Merrill, 1956).
28. UN/46/PV.41, Statement of Mr. Kofi Awoonor, representative of Ghana speaking on behalf of the group of 77. Quoted in Dallmeyer, "National Perspectives on Intervention," in Daniel & Hayes (eds.), *Beyond Traditional Peacekeeping* (London: Macmillan Press, 1995), p. 20.
29. Quoted in Freeman, "The Philosophical Foundations of Human Rights," *Human Rights Quarterly,* 16 (1994) p. 491.
30. R. J. Vincent, *Human Rights in International Relations,* p. 38. For an approach to human rights as expressing ethnocentrism, see Polis and Schwab, "Human Rights: A Western Construct with limited Applicability," in Polis and Schwab (eds.), *Human Rights Cultural and Ideological Perspective* (New York: Praeger, 1979).
31. Batailler Demichel, "Droits de l'homme et droits des peuples dans l'ordre international," in *Le Droit des Peuples à Disposer D'eux-mêmes. Mélanges offerts à Charles Chaumont* (Paris: Pédone, 1984), pp. 30–31.
32. "The Security Council shall, where appropriate, utilize such regional arrangements or agencies for enforcement action under its authority. But no enforcement action shall be taken under regional arrangements or by regional agencies without the authorization of the Security Council."
33. "The Security Council shall at all times be kept fully informed of activities undertaken or in contemplation under regional arrangements or by regional agencies for the maintenance of international peace and security."

34. Bruno Simma (ed.), *The Charter of the United Nations: A Commentary* (Oxford and New York: Oxford University Press, 2002), pp. 52–61.

35. Article 2 of the ECOWAS Treaty, 28 May 1975.

36. ECOWAS completed its structure with the Protocol on Non-Aggression of April 22, 1978 and the Protocol Relating to Mutual Assistance on Defence signed on May 29, 1981.

37. Article 52 (2) states: "The Members of the United Nations entering into such arrangements or constituting such agencies shall make every effort to achieve pacific settlement of local disputes through such regional arrangements or by such regional agencies before referring them to the Security Council."

38. Duke Simon, "The State and Human Rights: Sovereignty versus Humanitarian Intervention," *International Relations* 12 (1994), pp. 25–48.

39. *The Responsibility to Protect*, p. 54.

40. The legal maxim says "Minime mutanda sunt quae certam habuerunt interpretationem."

41. Bryan A. Garner, *Black's Law Dictionary,* 7th edition, p. 1318.

42. Article 28 reads: "Unless a different intention appears from the treaty or is otherwise established, its provision do not bind a party in relation *to any act* or fact which took place or any situation which ceased to exist before the date of the entry into force of the treaty with respect to the party."

43. Murphy, *Humanitarian Intervention,* p. 163; David Wippman, *Enforcing Restraint,* p. 75.

44. UN Department of Public Information Reference Paper, *The United Nations and Situation in Liberia* (April 1995). Quoted in Murphy, *Humanitarian Intervention,* p. 164.

45. Adekeye Adebajo, *Liberia's Civil War,* p. 48.

46. Two schools of International Relations (international society and regimes theories) recognize the need for limited joint hegemony or even for leadership by a single hegemon. For regimes theories, see S. D. Krasner, *International Regimes* (Ithaca: Cornell University Press, 1983); S. Haggard and B. A. Simmons, "Theories of International Regimes," *International Organization* 41/3 (1987), pp. 491–517; David Armstrong, *Revolution and World Order: The Revolutionary State in International Society* (Oxford: Clarendon Press 1993), p. 299–311.

47. Adekeye Adebajo, *Liberia's Civil War,* p. 45

48. Ibid, p. 48.

49. John Stremlau, *The International Politics of the Nigerian Civil War,* 1967–1970 (Princeton: Princeton University Press, 1977), p. 12.

50. K. B. Asante, "ECOWAS/CEAO: Conflict and cooperation in West Africa," in Ralph I. Onwuka and Amadu Sesay (eds.), *The Future of Regionalism in Africa* (New York: St. Martin's Press, 1985), p. 83.

51. Text of President Babangida's address to media in Lagos reprinted in *West Africa,* 6–12 August 1990, p. 2230.

52. For an extensive account on the relationship between the two presidents and their administrations, see Ademola Adeleke, "The Politics and Diplomacy of Peacekeeping in West Africa: The ECOWAS Operation in Liberia," *The*

Journal of Modern African Studies, 33, 4 (1995) pp. 576–579. The author notes for his argumentation that Doe was a personal friend of Babangida who paid US $20 million to establish the Ibrahim Babangida School of Political Science and Strategic Studies in Monrovia. Furthermore during the rapid advance of the armed groups on Monrovia, the only country Doe visited was Nigeria, with a request for arms.

53. Sola Akinrinade and Amadu Sesay (eds.), *Africa in The Post-Cold War International System*, (London; Washington: Printer, 1998), p. 57.

54. Ibid. p. 59.

55. For an example of such relationship, Joseph Momoh, the Sierra Leonean leader, was a classmate of Babangida.

56. Ayo Okukotun, "Authoritarian State, Crisis of Democratization And the Underground Media in Nigeria," *African Affairs*, (2002), p. 317.

57. A. Apter, "Nigeria, democracy and the politics of illusion," in J. L. and J. Comaroff (eds.), *Civil Society and the Political Imagination in Africa: Critical Perspectives* (Chicago: University of Chicago Press, 1999), pp. 267–307; Claude Ake, "The Nigerian State: Antinomies of a Periphery Formation," in Claude Ake, (ed.), *The Political Economy of Nigeria*, (London; New York: Longman, 1985); *Amnesty International*, "Nigeria: Time for Justice and Accountability," Dec. 21, 2000.

58. Larry Diamond, Anthony Kirk-Greene and Oyeleye Oyediran (eds.), *Transition Without End: Nigerian Politics and Civil Society Under Babangida* (Boulder, CO, : Lynne Rienner, 1997); Kunle Amuwo, Daniel Bach and Yann Lebeau (eds.), *Nigeria during the Abacha Years 1993–1998: The Domestic and international politics of democratization* (Ibadan: IFRAN, 2001), pp. 1–56.

NOTES TO CHAPTER THREE

1. The NPFL, for example, spawned The Independent National Patriotic Front of Liberia (INPFL) as well as the Central Revolutionary Council. A new group, ULIMO (the United Movement for Democracy and Liberation in Liberia), emerged in 1991 and later fragmented into factions (ULIMO-J and ULIMO-L led respectively by Roosevelt Johnston and Alhaji Kromah).

2. Kofi Annan, "Small Arms, Big Problems," *International Herald Tribune*, 10 July 2001.

3. Aboagye Festus, *ECOMOG: a subregional experience in conflict resolution and peacekeeping in Liberia*, pp. 43–55.

4. Report of the Inter-Agency Mission to West Africa "Towards a Comprehensive Approach to Durable and Sustainable Solutions to Priority Needs and Challenges in West Africa," UN Security Council document, 4/2001/434, p. 20.

5. S/1998/1096, Final Report of the International Commission of Inquiry (Rwanda), 18 November 1998, Para. 88.

6. Bayart J. F., Ellis S. and B. Hibou, *La criminalisation de l'Etat en Afrique* (Paris: Edition Complexe, 1997). For a detailed examination of warlordism

in Liberia, see Paul B. Rich, "Warlords, State Fragmentation and Dilemma of humanitarian intervention," *Small Wars and Insurgencies,* Vol. 10, no. 1 (Spring 1999), pp. 78–96.

7. J. Hirsch, *Sierra Leone: Diamonds and the Struggle for Democracy* (Boulder and London: Lynne Rienner Publishers, 2001).

8. On the benefits of the war for all actors involved in the conflict see among others: "Liberia: Sparking Fires in West Africa," *Africa Confidential* 32, (17 May 1991), p. 3; William Reno, *Warlords politics and African states* (Boulder and London: Lynne Rienner, 1998), pp. 104–105; Phillippa Atkinson, *The War Economy in Liberia: A Political Analysis* (London: Overseas Development Institute, 1997).

9. Herbert M. Howe, "Private security forces and Africa stability: the case of Executives Outcomes," *The Journal of Modern African Studies,* 36, (1998), pp. 313–314.

10. Eric G. Berman and Katie E. Sams, *Peacekeeping in Africa: Capabilities and Culpabilities* (Geneva: United Nations for Disarmament Research, 1997), p. 20.

11. Report of the Inter-Agency Mission to West Africa, 2 May, 2001.

12. UN Document A/52/871 and S/1998/318, "The causes of conflict and the promotion of durable peace and sustainable development in Africa," Report of the Secretary General, 13 April 1998, Para. 41; William Reno, *Warlord politics and African states;* Michael Bratton "Beyond the state: civil society and associational life in Africa," *World Politics* (1989), pp. 407–30.

13. C. Smith and A. Vines, *Light Weapons Proliferation in Southern Africa* (London: Centre for Defence 1997), No. 42, pp. 4–5.

14. Eric G. Berman and Katie E. Sams, *Peacekeeping in Africa,* p. 21.

15. ECOWAS Standing Mediation Committee, Decision A/Dec. 1/8/1990, on the Cease-fire and Establishment of an ECOWAS Cease-fire Monitoring Group for Liberia, Banjul, Republic of Gambia.

16. Quoted by Clement E. Adibe, "Coercive Diplomacy and the Third World," p. 12.

17. See Anthony C. Ofodile "The legality of ECOWAS intervention in Liberia," *Columbia Journal of Transnational Law,* 32 (1994).

18. Clement Adibe, *Disarmament and Conflict Resolution in Liberia* (Geneva: UNIIR Publication, 1996), p. 15.

19. Amadu Sesay, (ed.), *Africa in the Post Cold War.* The author is right in making this point because Article 16 of ECOWAS Protocol stipulate that in the event of aggression against a member state, "the head of the country shall send a written request for assistance to the present Chairman of the Authority of ECOWAS . . . the request shall mean that the authority is duly notified and the AAFC are placed under a state of emergency."

20. Ibid.

21. Article 2 of the ECOWAS Protocol on Non-Aggression reads: "Each Member State shall refrain from committing, encouraging or condoning acts of subversion, hostility or aggression against the territorial integrity or political independence of other Member States."

22. Article 4 reads: "Each Member State shall undertake to prevent non-resident foreigners from using its territory as a base for committing the acts referred to in Article 2 above against the sovereignty and territorial integrity of Member States."

23. Article 2 of ECOWAS Protocol relating to Mutual Assistance on Defense, signed on May 29 states: "Member States to declare and accept that any armed threat or aggression directed against any Member State shall constitute a threat or aggression against the entire community."

24. Article 3 of the Protocol.

25. Article 4 of the Protocol.

26. Article 4 (a) of the Protocol.

27. Article 4 (b) of the Protocol.

28. Article 18–2 of the Protocol.

29. Article 4 (b).

30. Article 15 states: "the legitimate defense of the territories of the Community shall in all cases justify Intervention by AAFC and shall therefore be carried out in accordance with the mechanism described in Articles 16, 17 and 18 below."

31. Cathal J. Nolan, *Greenwood Encyclopedia of International Relations*, (Greenwood Pub Group: Vol. I), 2002, p. 1.

32. Letter addressed by President Samuel K. Doe to the Chairman and Members of the Ministerial Meeting of the ECOWAS Standing Mediation Committee, 14 July 1990. Text reprinted in Weller, *The Liberian Crisis*, p. 32.

33. Doe's Criticism of Côte d'Ivoire; Burkina Faso Denies Involvement. BBC Monitoring Report, January 1990. Reprinted in M. Weller, p. 33.

34. Clement Adibe "The Liberian conflict and the ECOWAS-UN partnership," *Third World Quarterly*, vol. 18 (1997) and W. Ofuatey-Kodjoe, "Regional Organizations and the Resolution of Internal Conflict: The ECOWAS Intervention in Liberia," *International Peacekeeping* vol. 1, no. 3, Autumn 1994.

35. Ibid.,

36. Article 4 of the Treaty of the Economic Community of West African States, 28 May 1975.

37. Article 5–1.

38. Article 5–3.

39. However, we should also note that constitutive documents of the organization limit the power of the Authority of Heads of State and Government and some uncertainties remain: the rule of unanimity seems to be a *de facto* practice rather than a requirement in the decision-making process. See Samuel K. B. Asante, *The political economy of regionalism in Africa: a decade of the Economic Community of West African States* (New York: Praeger, 1986), pp. 69–73. If this is correct the inability of Liberia to participate in decision-making during the time of the crisis should not constitute a bar to decisions under the unanimity rule.

40. Article 9.

41. Here the Court restated Article 3, paragraph (g), of the definition of aggression annexed to General Assembly resolution 3314.

42. ICJ, Nicaragua, para. 94.
43. ICJ, Nicaragua Case, para. 95.

NOTES TO CHAPTER FOUR

1. These were the Bamako Ceasefire of November 1990, the Banjul Joint Statement of December 1990, the February 1991 Lomé Agreement, and the Yamoussoukro I-IV Accords of June-October 1991.
2. Adeleke, "The Politics and Diplomacy of Peacekeeping in West Africa," p. 580.
3. See Joint Declaration on Cessation of Hostilities and Peaceful Settlement of Conflict, Bamako, Republic of Mali, 28 November 1990.
4. See Liberia's Interim Government Proposal, 2 February 1991.
5. Charles Taylor has condemned the Nigerian government's military action and described it as an act of aggression against the Liberian People and has demanded the immediate and unconditional withdrawal of the Nigeria's government's military war machine from the Liberian soil.
6. The four others were the Presidents of Nigeria, Gambia, Togo and Burkina Faso.
7. See the communiqué of the meeting held in Yamoussoukro, 29–30 June 1991. *Official Journal of the Economic Community of West African States* (ECOWAS), November 1992.
8. *Africa Confidential* 32, no. 23 (22 November 1991) p. 6.
9. Adekeye Adebajo, *Liberia's Civil War,* p. 88.
10. Sawyer, who was not a warlord, was present at the meeting. Apart from the Committee members, Ghana, Nigeria, Mali, Burkina Faso and an INN representative attended the meeting. See the Committee's Final Communiqué, Yamoussoukro, and 17 September 1991. Text in *Official Journal of the Economic Community of West African States (ECOWAS),* November 1992.
11. Final Communiqué of the Fourth Meeting of the Committee of Five of the Economic Community of West African States on the Liberian Crisis, Yamoussoukro, 29–30 October 1991, point 7.
12. Ibid, point 6.
13. Ibid, point 6.
14. Adekeye Adebajo, *Building peace in West Africa,* pp. 54–55.
15. Eboe Hutchful, "Peacekeeping Under Conditions of Resource Stringency: Ghana's Army in Liberia," in Jakkie Cilliers and Greg Mills (eds.), *From Peacekeeping to Complex Emergencies: Peace Support Missions in Africa* (Johannesburg and Pretoria: South African Institute of International Affairs and Institute for Security Studies, 1999), p. 107.
16. See Cotonou Accord, 25 July 1993. Article 2 stipulates that the Parties agree to the ceasefire and the cessation of hostilities effective seven days from the date of signing; article 3 stipulates that ECOMOG and UN Observer Mission shall supervise and monitor the implementation of the agreement.

17. Cotonou Accord article 4.
18. Cotonou Accord articles 5, 6, 7.
19. Cotonou Accord articles 14 (1).
20. According to article 14 (7) of the Cotonou Accord, the two remaining members shall be selected in accordance with the following procedure: each of the parties shall nominate three eminent Liberians who together shall select two of their number to be additional members of the Council.
21. Cotonou Accord 14 (9).
22. Article 14 (8).
23. Cotonou Accord article 16 (4).
24. C. A. Alao, "Commentary on the Accords," in *Accord: An International Review of Peace Initiatives*, Issue I, 1996, p. 70.
25. On this point see Samuel Kofi Woods, Civic Initiatives in the Peace Process, available on the Internet at www.cr.org/accord/accord1/woods.htm. The author highlights the point that international negotiators provided tacit legitimation of violence and marginalized civic initiatives and called for civic roles in the peace process.
26. See Alao, "Commentary on the Accords," p. 71.
27. On the economic dimensions of the war and the intra-factional strife for diamonds, rubber and other commodities, see: Stephen Ellis, *The Mask of Anarchy. The Destruction of Liberia and the Religious Dimension of an African Civil War* (New York: New York University Press, 1999), p. 120. On markets and rackets, see p. 164. On the relations between rebels and armed groups with Western countries, see pp. 164–169. On ECOMOG involvement in the same business and interests involving military intelligence, officers, commanders and generals, see pp. 174–179 and on Nigeria import and export of heroin see, pp. 171–72.
28. Akosombo Agreement (Supplement to the Cotonou Accord), September 1994, Article 4.
29. Ibid. Art 14.
30. Ibid. Art 14 (vii).
31. Interview with Desk officer for Liberia, Department of Political Affairs, Africa Division, United Nations, New York June 2002.
32. Abuja Accord, 19 August 1995.
33. All parties to the first agreement signed the revised Abuja accord.
34. He confessed that he was a failure as chairman, but blamed it on the collective nature of the government. See "Liberia: Another Chance for Peace," *News Watch*, 9 September 1996, p. 24.
35. Martin Lowenkopf, "Liberia: Putting The State Back Together," in *Collapsed States*, p. 105.
36. Terrence Lyons, *Voting for Peace: Post Conflict Elections in Liberia* (Washington D.C.: Brookings Institution, 1999), p. 51.
37. Ibid, p. 57.
38. Fareed Zakaria, "The rise of illiberal democracy," *Foreign Affairs* 76 (November/December 1997) pp. 23–43.
39. Ibid, p. 25.

40. Article 25 of the new treaty envisioned six cases when member states can intervene. Those are: in cases of aggression or conflict in any member state or threat thereof; in cases of conflict between two or several Member States; in cases of internal conflict that threatens to trigger a humanitarian disaster or that poses a serious threat to peace and security in the sub-region; in the event of an overthrow or attempted overthrow of a democratically elected government; and in any other situation as may be decided by the Mediation and Security Council. This article contrasts with Article 18 (2) of the Protocol Relating to Mutual Assistance on Defense (PMAD), which states that "Community forces shall not intervene if the conflict remains purely internal." See developments in chapter 3.

41. Chapter IV of the treaty establishes a sub-regional security observation known as the Early Warning System for Conflict Prevention.

42. Paul F. Diehl, *International Peacekeeping* (Baltimore: The Johns Hopkins University Press, 1993), chapter 1.

43. See chapter 3 of the Protocol on Mutual Assistance and Defense.

44. In the new Mechanism, peacekeeping is defined at Article 51 as "all forms of military intervention to be undertaken by ECOWAS." This suggests a wide definition to include enforcement actions as discussed during the Meeting of the Ministers of Defense, Internal Affairs and Security held in Banjul in 1998.

45. See chapter 3 and developments on the First Session of the SMC

46. See chapter 3

47. See Article 22 (c).

48. Article 6 reads: "The Authority shall be the Mechanism's highest decision-making body." Under the second paragraph, it defines its powers: "It shall have power to act on all matters concerning conflict prevention, management and resolution, peacekeeping, security, humanitarian support, peace building , (. . .) as well as all other matters covered by the provisions of this Mechanism."

49. Article 7.

50. Article 10.

51. Personal discussions with Margaret Vogt who headed the team of experts in Banjul and with Dr. Mohammed Ibn Chambas Executive Secretary of ECOWAS at a forum discussion organized by International Peace Academy. New York, 29 April 2002.

52. Article 52 (1) states that "Nothing in the present Charter precludes the existence of regional arrangements or agencies for dealing for such matters relating to the maintenance of international peace and security as are appropriate for regional action, provided that such arrangements and agencies and their activities are consistent with the Purposes and Principles of the United Nations."

53. Article 53 is clear: "The Security Council shall, where appropriate, utilize such regional arrangements or agencies for enforcement action under its authority. But no enforcement action shall be taken under regional arrangements or by regional agencies without the authorization of the Security Council."

54. See claims arguing that the Security Council approved ECOWAS' intervention in Liberia *ex post facto* in J. A. Frowein, "Legal Consequences of International Law Enforcement in the Case of Security Council Inaction," in J. Delbruck (ed.), *The Future of International Law Enforcement: New Scenarios-New Law?* (Berlin: Duncker & Humblot, 1992), p. 122.

55. Article 103 of the UN Charter states: "In the event of a conflict between the obligations of the Members of the United Nations under the present Charter and their obligations under any other international agreement, their obligations under the present Charter shall prevail."

56. Article 24 (1) of the UN Charter states: "In order to ensure prompt and effective action by the United Nations, its members confer on the Security Council primary responsibility for the maintenance of international peace and security, and agree that in carrying out its duties under this responsibility the Security Council acts on their behalf."

57. Article 53 (1).

58. Since the outbreak of the Gulf War, the Security Council has become very flexible in citing Chapter VII. It has extended the notion of threat to international peace in different and somehow controversial situations. This was done in Resolution 733 (1992) on Somalia; Resolution 748 (1992) concerning Libya's failure to renounce terrorism; Resolution 841 as regard to Haiti or Resolution 1054 (1996) prompted by Sudan's non-compliance with demands for extradition of suspected "terrorists."

59. P. Malanczuk, *Akehurst's Modern Introduction to International Law* 7th edition, 1997, p. 426.

60. H. Kelsen, *The Law of the United Nations: A Critical Analysis of its Fundamental Problems* (New York: Praeger, 1966), p. 727.

61. See, *The Responsibility To Protect*, pp. 47–55.

NOTES TO CHAPTER FIVE

1. Boutros Boutros-Ghali, *Contribution à l'étude des ententes régionales* (Paris: Editions A. Pédone, 1949).

2. Boutros Boutros-Ghali, *An Agenda for Peace* (New York, United Nations, 1992), p. 37.

3. In 1995 the Secretary General received two requests to deal with the question of greater cooperation and support of regional organizations in Africa. The first was in the form of a Presidential Statement from the Security Council and the second a request from the Special Committee on Peacekeeping Operations.

4. S/PRST/1997/46, 25 September 1997.

5. "The causes of conflict and the promotion of durable peace and sustainable development in Africa," Report of the Secretary General, A/52/871-S/1998/138, 13 April 1998, Para. 5.

6. Among these are the Special Committee on Peacekeeping Operations and the United Nations Lessons Learned Unit, Cooperation between the

United Nations and Regional Organizations/Arrangement in a Peacekeeping Environment, Suggested Principles and Mechanisms, March 1999.

7. "Implementation of the recommendations of the Special Committee on Peacekeeping Operations, Report of the Secretary General," A/54/670, 6 January 2000, Para. 90.

8. SC/6734, 29 September 1999.

9. January 2000.

10. Report of the Panel on United Nations Peace Operations, 23 August 2000, Para. 54.

11. Chapter VII of the UN Charter and actions with respect to threat to the peace, breaches of peace, and acts of aggression especially articles 39, 41 and 42.

12. Daniel Bach, "Institutional Crisis and the Search of New Models," in Réal Lavergne (ed.), *Regional Integration and Cooperation in West Africa* (Trenton, N.J., and Asmara, Eritrea: Africa World Press, 1997), p. 87. On financial difficulties as undermining the capabilities of West African states see also Eric G. Berman and Katie E. Sams, *Peacekeeping in Africa,* p. 146. For a country-by-country review on political economic and other related issues, see *Africa Contemporary Record: Annual Survey and Documents* (Volume 23).

13. Eric G. Berman and Katie E. Sams, *Peacekeeping in Africa,* p. 146.

14. Samir Amin, *Neocolonialism in West Africa* (New York and London: Monthly Review Press, 1973); Robert Bates, *Markets and States in Tropical Africa* (Berkeley, Los Angeles, and London: University of California Press, 1981).

15. RFI, Jeudi 19 décembre 2002, "Sommet de Dakar: grandes ambitions, faible mobilisation;" RFI, 21 Janvier 2003, "La CEDEAO dans l'impasse: quatre mois après le début de la rébellion, la CEDEAO a été conduit à avouer son impuissance."

16. Stephen Smith, "Au Togo, la présidence à vie devient constitutionnelle." *Le Monde,* Mardi 31 décembre 2002.

17. Adekeye Adebajo, *Building Peace in West Africa,* pp. 111–136 and Eric G. Berman and Katie E. Sams, *Peacekeeping in Africa,* pp.128–138.

18. Carolyn M. Shaw and Julius O. Ihvonbere, "Hegemonic Participation in Peace-Keeping Operations: The Case of Nigeria and ECOMOG," *International Journal on World Peace* 13/2 (1996), pp. 42–43.

19. Quoted in Clement E. Adibe, "The Liberian conflict and the ECOWAS-UN partnership" *Third World Quarterly* (1997), p. 483.

20. Robert Mortimer, "Sénégal's Role in ECOMOG: The Francophone Dimension," *Journal of Modern African Studies,* 34/2 (1996).

21. "Hegemonic Participation in Peace Keeping Operations: The Case of Nigeria and ECOMOG," p. 48.

22. Ibid; p. 51.

23. Jeffrey Goldberg, "A War without Purpose in a Country without Identity," *New York Times Magazine,* (January 22, 1995), p. 37.

24. Andrew Hurrell, "France: Adjustment to Change," in Hedley Bull (ed.), *The Expansion of International Society* (Oxford: Clarendon Press, 1984),

p. 337; see also J. F. Bayart, *La Politique Africaine de François Mitterrand* (Paris: Karthala, 1984).

25. Quoted in Gowon, *Economic Community of West Africa States*, p. 239; S. K. B. Asante, "ECOWAS/CEAO: Conflict and Cooperation in West Africa," in R. I. Onwuka and A. Sesay (eds.), *The Future of Regionalism in West Africa*, pp. 86–87; Daniel Bach, "The Politics of West African Cooperation: CEAO and ECOWAS," *Journal of Modern African Studies* 21/4 (1983).

26. A. Dumoulin, *La France militaire et l'Afrique* (Bruxelles: GRIP/Complexe 1997).

27. "Continuity and Change in Franco-African Relations," *Journal of Modern African Studies* 33/1 (1995), p. 6.

28. Rebellion in Cote d'Ivoire, *World Press Review*, February 2003.

29. RFI, "Sommet de Dakar: Grandes Ambitions, Faible Mobilisation," Jeudi 19 décembre 2002.

30. Le Monde, "Le gouvernement ivoirien accuse les rebelles de violer le cessez-le-feu," Vendredi 17 janvier 2003.

31. Le Monde, "Les rebelles de L'Ouest signent un cessez-le-feu avec la France," Mercredi 8 janvier 2003; Le Figaro, " Rebelles ivoiriens et soldats français cessent le feu," Mercredi 8 janvier 2003.

32. All Africa, "Ivory Coast Foes Gather in Paris for crucial peace," January 15, 2003.

33. Report of the Inter-Agency Mission to West Africa, "Toward a comprehensive approach to durable and sustainable solutions to priority needs and challenges in West Africa," S/2001/434, 30 April 2001, Para 5.

34. Ibid, 96.

35. Ibid, 101.

36. RFI, "Les rebelles accusent le Ghana de soutenir militairement Gbagbo," Lundi 25 Novembre 2002.

37. Resolution 1343 of March 7 2001demands " . . . that the Government of Liberia immediately ceases its support for the RUF in Sierra Leone and other armed rebel groups in the region, and particularly take the following concrete steps: (a) expel all RUF members from Liberia . . . (b) cease all financial and, in accordance with resolution 1171 (1998), military support to the RUF, including all transfers of arms and ammunition, all military training and the provision of logistical and communications support; (c) cease all direct or indirect import of Sierra Leone rough diamonds. For successive violations, see, Le Figaro, "Ces mercenaires libériens qui se battent en Côte d'Ivoire," Mercredi 8 Janvier 2003.

38. Le Parisien, "Gbagbo finira devant le Tribunal Pénal International," 21 Janvier 2003.

NOTES TO CHAPTER SIX

1. See, for example, Margaret Vogt, (ed.), *A Bold Attempt at Regional Peacekeeping: ECOMOG and the Liberian Crisis*, Adekeye Adebajo, *Building Peace in West Africa*. Academic articles have also adopted the

same approach, see among others, Abiodun Alao, "Peace Keeping in Sub-Saharan Africa The Liberian Civil War," in Michael Clarke (ed.), *Brassey's Defense Yearbook,* (London: Brassey's Publishers, 1993); Funmi Olonisakin, "African Home-Made Peacekeeping Initiatives" *Armed Forces and Society,* 23/3 (Spring 1997).

2. Anthony Daniel, *Monrovia Mon Amour* (London: John Murray, 1992), p. 28.

3. Harold D. Nelson (ed.), *Liberia: A Country Study* (Washington DC: American University 1985); Hiram Ruiz, *Uprooted Liberians: Casualties of a Brutal War* (Washington, DC: U.S. Committee for Refugees, 1992).

4. H. D. Nelson (ed.), *Liberia: A Country Study* (Washington, DC: American University, 1985), pp. 43–45.

5. Max Weber, "The fundamental Concepts of Sociology," in Talcott Parsons, (ed.), *The Theory of Social and Economic Organization* (New York: Free Press, 1964), p. 156.

6. Christopher Clapham, *Africa and the International System: The politics of state survival* (Cambridge: Cambridge University Press, 1996); Robert Jackson, *Quasi-States: Sovereignty, International Relations and the Third World* (Cambridge: Cambridge University Press, 1990).

7. Richard Joseph, *Democracy and Prebendal Politics in Nigeria: The Rise and Fall of The Second Republic* (New York: Cambridge University Press, 1987); Thomas Callaghy, *The State-Society Struggle: Zaire in Comparative Perspective* (New York: Columbia University Press, 1984). For a summary until the mid-nineties see Michael Bratton and Nicolas Van De Walle, "Neopatrimonial Regimes and Political Transitions in Africa," *World Politics,* vol. 46, No. 4 (July 1994), pp. 453–489.

8. Robert Jackson and Carl G. Rosberg, "Why Africa's Weak States Persist: The Empirical and the Juridical in Statehood," in Atul Kohli (ed.), *The State and Development in the Third World* (Princeton, N.J.: Princeton University Press, 1986), pp. 259–282.

9. Fred Riggs, "The Nation State and Other Actors," in James Rosenau, *International Politics and Foreign Policy* (New York, The Free Press, 1969) p. 90.

10. *West Africa,* 9 June 1980, p. 1007.

11. Peter Ayang, "Alliance and State in Liberia," in Peter Ayang (ed.), *Popular Struggles for Democracy in Africa* (London and New Jersey: Zed and UNU, 1987), p. 209.

12. See Ruiz, *Uprooted Liberians,* p. 4. Many believed that Jackson F. Doe (no relation to the president) of the Liberian Action Party won. Jackson Doe was the son of a Gio from Nimba, who had been recruited by Quiwonkpa to work in the government.

13. Brenda M. Branaman, *Liberia: Issues for the United States* (Washington, DC: Congressional Research Services, 1991).

14. Edward D. Mansfield and Jack Snyder, "Democratization and the danger of war," *International Security,* 20 (1995), pp. 5–38.

15. Joel Migdal, *Strong Societies and Weak States: State-Society Relations and State Capabilities in the Third World* (Princeton, NJ: Princeton University Press, 1988), pp. 227–229.

16. Catherine Boone, *Political topographies of the African state: territorial authority and institutional choice* (Cambridge, U.K.; New York: Cambridge University Press, 2003); Catherine Boone, "States in Ruling Classes in Postcolonial Africa: The Enduring Contradictions of Power," in J. Migdal, J. Kholi and V. Shue (eds.), *State Power and Social Forces: Domination and Transformation in the Third World* (Cambridge: Cambridge University Press, 1994).

17. Lin Yutang, *My Country, My People* (New York: The John Day Company, Inc., 1939), pp. 48–49.

18. Ibrahim Abdullah, "Bush path to destruction: the origin and character of the Revolutionary United Front/Sierra Leone," *The Journal of Modern African Studies*, 36/ 2 (1998), pp. 203–235.

19. Yusuf Bangura, "Understanding the political and cultural dynamics of the Sierra Leone War: a critique of Paul Richards' *Fighting for the Rain Forest*," *African Development*, 22 /2 (1997).

20. Olivier Hurley, *Conflict in Africa* (London: Tauris Academic Studies 1995).

21. Berkeley Bill, *Liberia: A Promise Betrayed* (New York, Lawyers Committee on Human Rights, 1986), p. 25.

22. Emmanuel Dolo, *Democracy Versus Dictatorship: The Quest of Freedom and Justice in Africa's oldest Republic-Liberia* (Maryland: University Press of America, 1996), p. 65.

23. *Ghanaian Chronicle* (Accra), January 17, 2003, "After Rebel Truce, Eyadema Asks, Which Country Next?"

24. I thank Masse Ndiaye for this point and his insightful comments on this chapter.

25. See, among others: "Liberia: Court ruling in human rights," in *Amnesty International*, September 1992; "Liberia: New Accounts Detail Abuses," *Human Rights Watch Africa*, Press Release March 6, 2003.

26. Andrew Hurrell, "Explaining the Resurgence of Regionalism in World Politics," *Review of International Studies* 21(4), pp. 331–358; Louise Fawcett and Andrew Hurrell, *Regionalism in World Politics. Regional Organization and International Order* (Oxford: Oxford University Press, 1995).

27. Mohamed Ayoob, "Regional Security and the Third World," In M. Ayoob (ed.), *Regional Security in the Third World: Case Studies from Southeast Asia and the Middle East* (Boulder, Co: Westview Press, 1986).

28. Mohamed Ayoob, *The Third World Security Predicament: State Making, Regional Conflict, and the International System* (Boulder: Lynne Reinner, 1995).

29. Zartman uses the term "state collapse" to describe the failure of good governance, law and order. Robert H. Jackson refers to failed states as states that are internationally recognized as sovereign territories, but which nevertheless incapable of providing those domestic conditions of peace, order and good government.

30. William Zartman, *Collapsed States*, p. 5.

31. For an articulation of the concept with reference to Africa, see Roger Charlton and Roy May, "warlords and militarism in Chad," *Review of African Political Economy*, 45/46 (1989), pp. 12–25.

32. Robert Kaplan, "The Coming Anarchy: how scarcity, crime, overpopulation and disease are rapidly destroying the social fabric of our planet," *Atlantic Monthly,* February 1994, pp. 48; Jean-Christophe Rufin, *L'Empire et Les Nouveaux Barbares* (Paris: Lattés, 1991).
33. UN Document A/52/871-S/1998/318. "The causes of conflicts and the promotion of durable peace and sustainable development in Africa: Report of the Secretary General," 13 April 1998, Para. 12.
34. The Causes of conflicts and the promotion of durable peace, Para. 41.
35. Robert I. Rotberg, "Africa's Mess, Mugabe's Mayhem," *Foreign Affairs* September/October (2000), p. 47.
36. Jean Francois Bayart, Stephen Ellis, Beatrice Hibou, *The Criminalization of the State in Africa* (Oxford: International African Institute in association with J. Curey, Oxford, Bloomington: Indiana University Press, 1999).
37. Patrick Chabal, Jean Pascal-Daloz, *Africa works: disorder as political instrument* (Oxford: International African Institute in association with J. Curey, Oxford, Bloomington: Indiana University Press, 1999).
38. James G. March and Johan P. Olsen, *Democratic Governance* (New York: Free Press, 1995), pp. 45–47.
39. World Bank, *Sub-Saharan Africa: From Crisis to Sustainable Growth* (Washington D.C., The World Bank Group Publications), p. 60.
40. March and Olsen, p. 49.

NOTES TO THE CONCLUSION

1. Emmanuel Kwesi Aning, "The International Dimensions of Internal Conflict: The Case of Nigeria and West Africa," Copenhagen Centre for Development Research, Working Paper 97/4 (June 1997), p. 12.
2. Roberts Adams, "A New Age in international relations?" *International Affairs,* 67/3 (1991), 524–525.
3. Jarat Chopra and Thomas G. Weiss, "Sovereignty is no longer sacrosanct: codifying humanitarian intervention," *Ethics and International Affairs,* 6 (1992), pp. 102–103.
4. James Leslie Brierly, *The Law of Nations* (New York: Oxford University Press, 6th ed. 1963), p. 1.
5. Mario Bettati, Bernard Kouchner, *Le devoir d'ingérence* (Paris: Denoël, 1987)
6. Quoted in Robert Jackson, *The Global Covenant,* p. 356.
7. *The Guardian,* 12 October 2001.
8. K. Watkins, "This Deal is Immoral, Mr. Blair," *The Guardian,* 21 December 2001.
9. Terry Nardin, "International ethics and international law," *Review of International Studies,* 18/ 1 (1992), p. 19.
10. Tian Jin, "Complexities of Human Rights in today's world," *Beijing Review,* 33 (May 28-June 3, 1990), 10–11.
11. Article 2 of the UN General Assembly on the Inadmissibility of Intervention in the Domestic Affairs of States and the Protection of their and their sovereignty and the 1986 *Nicaragua Case.*

12. William Reno, "The Business of War in Liberia," *Current History,* 95 (1996), p. 214. See also William Reno, *Warlord Politics and African States* (Boulder: Lynne Rienner Publishers, 1998).

13. Donald J. Puchala, *The Ethics of Globalism* (Providence: John W. Holmes Memorial Lecture Reports and Papers) no. 3, 1995.

14. *Human Rights Watch,* "UN Security Council Member Facilitates Atrocities," (New York, Nov 5, 2003).

15. Peter Takirambudde, "Liberia: where the arms come from," *International Herald Tribune,* Sept 17, 2003.

16. Cindy Shiner, "A Disarming Start," *Africa Report,* 39/3 (1994), pp. 62–4.

17. Robert Putnam, *Making Democracy Work* (Princeton, N.J.: Princeton University Press, 1993), p. 1993.

18. Robin Theobold, "Patrimonialism," *World Politics* 34 (1982), p. 549.

19. Mamadou Dia, *A Governance Approach to Civil Service Reform in Sub-Saharan Africa* World Bank Technical Paper Series 225.

20. Nicolas van de Walle, *African Economies and the Politics of Permanent Crisis: 1979–1989* (New York: Cambridge University Press, 2001), p.117.

Bibliography

Abdullah, I, "Bush Path to Destruction: The Origins and Character of the Revolutionary United Front," *Journal of Modern African Studies* 36 (2) 1998.

Abogaye, F, *ECOMOG: A Subregional Experience in Conflict Resolution, Management and Peacekeeping in Liberia* (Accra: Sedco Enterprise, 1999).

Adebajo, A, "Nigeria: Africa's New Gendarme?" *Security Dialogue* 31 (2) 2000.

———, *Liberia's Civil War: Nigeria, ECOMOG and Regional Security in West Africa* (Boulder and London: Lynne Rienner, 2003).

———, *West Africa Security Challenges* (Boulder and London: Lynne Rienner Publishers, 2004).

———, *Building Peace in West Africa: Liberia, Sierra Leone, and Guinea Bissau* (Boulder and London: Lynne Reinner, 2002).

———, Adebajo, Adekeye, and Chris Lamberg. "The Heirs of Nkrumah: Africa's New Interventionists," *Pugwash Occasional Paper* 2 (1) 2001.

Adelman, H, "The Ethics of Humanitarian Intervention," *Public Affairs Quarterly*, 6 (1), 1992.

Ademola, A, "The Politics and Diplomacy of Peacekeeping in West Africa: The ECOWAS Operation in Liberia," *The Journal of Modern African Studies*, 33 (4) 1995.

Aderinsola, M, "The Involvement of ECOWAS in Liberia's Peacekeeping," in Edmond J. Keller and D. Rothchild (eds.), *Africa in the New International Order. Rethinking State Sovereignty and Regional Security* (Boulder, Col.: Lynne Reinner, 1996)

Adibe, C, "The Liberian Conflict and the ECOWAS-UN Partnership," *Third World Quarterly* 18, (3) 1997.

———, *Disarmament and Conflict Resolution Project. Managing Arms in Peace Processes: Liberia* (Geneva: UNIDIR, 1996).

———, "Coercive Diplomacy and the Third World: Africa After the Cold War," Paper Presented to the Workshop on Coercive Diplomacy, King's College, London, 7–9 June 1995.

Africa Confidential, 32, November 1991.

Africa Confidential 39, no. 21 (October, 1998): "Militias and Markets Forces,"

Africa Confidential. Chronology of Sierra Leone from 1991 to 1998: How Diamonds Fueled the Conflict," http://www.africa-confidential.com/sandline.hml.

Africa Contemporary Record: Annual Survey and Documents, volume 23.

Ake, C, "The Nigerian State: Antinomies of a Periphery Formation," in Claude Ake (ed.), *The Political Economy of Nigeria* (London: Longman, 1985).

Akehurst, M, "Humanitarian Intervention," in Hedley Bull (ed.), *Intervention in World* Politics (Oxford: Clarendon Press, 1984).

Akinrinade, S, and Sesay, A, (ed.), *Africa in the Post-Cold War International System* (London; Washington: Pinter, 1998).

Alao, A, (ed.), *Peacekeepers, Politicians, and Warlords: The Liberian Peace Process* (NY: United Nations University Press, 1999).

———, "Commentary on the Accords," in *Accord: An International Review of Peace Initiatives,* 1, (1996).

———, "Peace Keeping in Sub-Saharan Africa: The Liberian Civil War," in Michael Clarke (ed.), *Brassey's Defense Yearbook* (London: Brassey's Publishers, 1993).

Amin, S, *Neocolonialism in West Africa* (New York and London: Monthly Review Press, 1973).

Amnesty International, *Amnesty International Report* (London: Amnesty International Publications, 1985).

———, *Amnesty International Report* (London: Amnesty International Publications, 1987).

———, *Amnesty International Report* (London: Amnesty International Publications, 1989).

———, *Amnesty International Report* (London: Amnesty International Publications, 1992).

———, *Amnesty International Report* (London: Amnesty International Publications, 2000).

Andrew, C, "France: Adjustment to Change," in Hedley Bull, (ed.), *The Expansion of International Society* (Oxford: Clarendon Press, 1984).

An-Naim, A, and Deng F, (eds.), *Human Right in Africa: Cross-Cultural Perspective* (Washington, DC: The Brookings Institution, 1990).

Annan, K, "Peacekeeping, Military Intervention and National Sovereignty in Internal Armed Conflict," in Jonathan Moore (ed.), *Hard Choices: Moral Dilemmas in Humanitarian Intervention* (New York: Rowman &Littlefield, 1998).

———, "Two Concepts of Sovereignty," *The Economist,* 18 September 1999.

———, "Small Arms, Big Problems," *International Herald Tribune* (10 July, 2001).

Apter, A, "Nigeria, democracy and the politics of illusion," in J. L. and J. Comaroff (eds.), *Civil Society and the Political Imagination in Africa: Critical Perspectives* (Chicago: University of Chicago Press, 1999).

Arend, A, and Beck, R, *International Law and the Use of Force* (London: Routledge, 1993).

Armstrong, D, *Revolution and World Order: The Revolutionary State in International Society* (Oxford: Clarendon Press, 1993).

Asante, S, K, "ECOWAS/CEAO: Conflict and Cooperation in West Africa," in R. I. Onwuka and A. Sesay (eds.), *The Future of Regionalism in West Africa* (London: Macmillan, 1985).

————, *The Political Economy of Regionalism in Africa: A Decade of the Economic Community of West African States* (New York: Praeger, 1986).

Atkinson, P, *The War Economy in Liberia: A Political Analysis* (London: Overseas Development Institute, 1997).

Ayang, P, "Alliance and State in Liberia," in Peter Ayang (ed.), *Popular Struggles for Democracy in Liberia* (London and New Jersey: ZED and UNU, 1987).

Ayo, O, "Authoritarian State, Crisis of Democratization and the Underground Media in Nigeria," *African Affairs* (2002).

Ayoob, M, "Regional Security and The Third World," in Mohamed Ayoob (ed.), *Regional Security in the Third World: Cases Studies from Southeast Asia and the Middle East* (Boulder, Co: Westview press, 1986).

————, Ayoob, M, *The Third World Security Predicament: State Making, Regional Conflict and the International System* (Boulder: Lynne Reinner, 1995).

Bach, D, "Institutional Crisis and the Search for New Models," in Réal Lavergne (ed.), *Regional Integration and Cooperation in Africa* (Trenton, N.J: Africa World Press; Ottawa: International Development Research Center, 1997)

————, "The Politics of West African Cooperation: CEAO and ECOWAS," *Journal of Modern African Studies* 21/4 (1983).

Bach, D, and Lebeau, Y, (eds.), *Nigeria during the Abacha Years (1993–1998): The Domestic and International Politics of Democratization* (Ibadan: IFRA, 2001).

Badie, B, and Birnbaum P, *The Sociology of the State* (Chicago: University of Chicago Press, 1983).

Badie, B, *Un monde sans souveraineté: Les Etats entre ruse et responsabilité* (Paris: Fayard, 1996).

Bangura, Y, "Understanding the political and the dynamics of the Sierra Leone War: A critique of Paul Richards' *Fighting for the Rain Forest*," *African Development*, 22 (1997).

Baranovsky, V, "Humanitarian Intervention: Russian Perspectives," *Pugwash Occasional Papers 2001.*

Barrett, Lindsay, "Why Sénégal withdrew," *West Africa* no. 3931 (25–31 January 1993).

Barzani, M, "Hope Restored: Benefits of Humanitarian Intervention," *Harvard International Review,* 16 (1) (1993).

Bates, R, *Markets and States in Tropical Africa* (Los Angeles and London: University of California Press, 1981).

Bayart, J, F, *La criminalisation de l'Etat en Afrique* (Paris: Editions Complexe, 1997).

Bazyler, M, "Reexamining the Doctrine of Humanitarian Intervention in Light of the Atrocities in Kampuchea and Ethiopia," *Stanford Journal of International Law,* (1987).

Beach H, "Do we need a doctrine of just intervention?" *Council for Arms Control* (London: Centre for Defense Studies, 1993).

Beitz, C, *Political Theory and International Relations* (Princeton: Princeton University Press, 1979).

Berman, E. G., and Katie E. Sams, *Peacekeeping in Africa: Capabilities and Culpabilities* (Geneva and Pretoria: UN Institute for Disarmament Research and Institute of Securities Studies, 2000).

Bettati M, and Kouchner, *Le Devoir d'ingérence* (Paris: Denoël, 1987).

Betts, R, "The Delusion of Impartial Intervention," *Foreign Affairs*, 73/6 (1993).

Bierly, J, *The Law of Nations* (New York: Oxford University Press, 6th ed. 1963).

Bill, B, *Liberia: A Promise Betrayed* (New York: Lawyers Committee for Human Rights, 1986).

Boone, C, "States in Ruling Classes in Postcolonial Africa: The Enduring Contradictions of Power," in Migdal, J. Kholi and Shue V, (eds.), *State Power and Social Forces: Domination and Transformation in the Third World* (Cambridge: Cambridge University Press, 1994).

Boutros Boutros-Ghali, *An Agenda for Peace* (New York: United Nations, 1992).

——, "Empowering the United Nations," *Foreign Affairs*, 71/2 (1992–93).

——, *Contribution à l'étude des ententes régionales* (Paris : Editions A. Pédone, 1949).

Bratton, M, "Towards Governance in Africa: Popular Demands and State Responses," in Goran Hyden and Bratton (eds.), *Governance and Politics in Africa* (Boulder: Lynne Reinner, 1991).

——, "Beyond the State: Civil Society and Associational Life in Africa," *World Politics* (1989)

Bratton, M., and Walle, V, "Neopatrimonial Regimes and Political Transitions in Africa," *World Politics*, vol. 46, 4 (1994).

Brenda, M. B., *Liberia: Issues for the United States* (Washington, DC: Congressional Research Services, 1991).

Brown, C, *Sovereignty, Rights and Justice* (Malden: Blackwell Publishers INC, 2002).

Brown, E, M, (ed.), *Ethnic Conflict and International Security* (Princeton: Princeton University Press, 1993).

——, *The International Dimensions of Internal Conflict* (Cambridge: The MIT Press, 1996).

Brown, S, *Human Rights in World Politics* (New York: Longman, 2000).

Brownlie, I, *Principles of Public International Law*, 5th edn. (Oxford: Clarendon Press, 1998).

Bull, H, (ed.), *Intervention in World Politics* (Oxford: Clarendon Press, 1984).

——, *The Anarchical Society*, 2nd edn. (London: Macmillan, 1995).

——, and Watson, A, (eds.), *The Expansion of International Society* (Oxford: Clarendon Press, 1984).

——, K. Kingsbury, and A. Roberts, (eds.), *Hugo Grotius and International Relations* (Oxford: Clarendon Press, 1990).

Buzan, B, *People, States, and Fear: An Agenda for International Security in the Post-Cold War Era* (Boulder: Lynne Reinner, 1991).

Callaghy, T, *The State-Society Struggle: Zaire in Comparative Perspective* (New York: Columbia University Press, 1984).

Calvo, C, *Le droit international et pratique précédé d'un exposé historique des progrès de la science du droit des gens*, 5th edn. (Paris: A. Rousseau, 1896).

Camilleri, J, A. and Falk, J, *The End of Sovereignty? The Politics of a Shrinking and Fragmenting World* (Brookfield, VT: Ashgate Publishing Company, 1992).

Caney, S, "Humanitarian Intervention and State Sovereignty," in Andrew Walls (ed.), *Ethics and International Affairs* (Oxford: Rowman & Littlefield, 2000).

Cassese, A, "*Ex iniuria ius oritur:* Are we moving towards International Legitimation of Forcible Humanitarian Countermeasures in the World Community?" *European Journal of International Law,* 10 (1999).

Chesterman, S, *Just War or Just Peace? Humanitarian Intervention and International Law* (Oxford: Oxford University Press, 2001).

———, "Law, Subject and Subjectivity in International Relations: International Law and the Postcolony," *Melbourne University Law Review,* 20 (1996).

Charlton R, and May, R, "Warlords and Militarism in Chad," *Review of African Political Economy,* 45/46 (1989).

Chipman, J, *French Power in Africa* (Oxford: Basil Blackwell, 1989).

Chopra, J, and Weiss, T, "Sovereignty is no longer sacrosanct: codifying humanitarian intervention," *Ethics and International Affairs,* 6 (1992).

Christenson, G, A., "The World Court and jus cogens," *American Journal of International Law,* 81 (1987).

Chukwuka, A, "The Legality of ECOWAS Intervention in Liberia," *Columbia Journal of Transnational Law,* 32/2 (1994).

Clapham, C, *Africa and the International System: The Politics of State Survival* (Cambridge: Cambridge University Press, 1996).

———, *Liberia and Sierra Leone: An Essay in Comparative Politics* (Cambridge: Cambridge University Press, 1976).

Comaroff, J, L., and Comaroff, Jean, *Civil Society and the Political Imagination in Africa: Critical Perspective* (Chicago: University of Chicago Press, 1999).

Cuéllar, J. P., *Report of the Secretary General on the Work of the Organization* (New York: United Nations, 1991).

D'Amato, Anthony, "The Invasion of Panama was a Lawful Response to Tyranny," *American Journal of International Law,* 84 (1990).

Damrosch, L, (ed.), *Enforcing Restraint: Collective Intervention in Internal Conflicts* (New York: Council on Foreign Relations Press, 1993).

Daniel, A, *Monrovia Mon Amour* (London: John Murray, 1992).

Daniel, D, and Hayes, B, C., *Beyond Traditional Peacekeeping* (London: Macmillan Press, 1995).

Danish Institute of International Affairs, *Humanitarian Intervention: Legal and Political Aspects* (Copenhagen: Danish Institute of International Affairs, 1999).

Demichel, B, "'Droits de l'homme et droits des peuples dans l'ordre international," in *Mélanges Offerts à Charles Chaumont: Le droit des peuples à disposer d'eux-mêmes. Méthodes d'analyse du droit international* (Paris: Pédone, 1984).

Diamond, L., Greene, K, A., and Oyediran, O, (eds.), *Transition Without End: Nigerian Politics and Civil Society Under Babangida* (Boulder: Lynne and Rienner, 1997).

Diehl, P, F., *International Peacekeeping* (Baltimore: The John Hopkins University Press, 1993).

Donnelly, J, *Universal Human Rights in Theory and Practice* (Ithaca: Cornell University Press, 1989).

Dumoulin, A, *La France militaire et l'Afrique* (Bruxelles: GRIP/Complexe, 1997).

Economic Community of West African States (ECOWAS), Treaty of 28 May 1975

————, ECOWAS Protocol on Non- Aggression, 22 April 1978

————, ECOWAS Protocol Relating to Mutual Assistance on Defense, 29 May 1981

————, First Session of the ECOWAS Standing Mediation Committee. Final Communiqué, Banjul, 6–7, 1990.

————, First Extraordinary Session of the Authority of Heads of State and Government. Final Communiqué. Bamako, 27–28 November 1990.

————, ECOWAS Final Communiqué of the First Meeting of the committee of Five on Liberia. Yamoussoukro, Côte d'Ivoire, 29 July 1991.

————, ECOWAS Peace Plans and Accords

————, Yamoussoukro I Accord (30 June 1991)

————, Yamoussoukro II Accord (29 July 1991)

————, Yamoussoukro III Accord (17 September 1991)

————, Yamoussoukro IV Accord (30 October 1991)

————, Geneva Ceasefire (17 July 1993)

————, Cotonou Accord (25 July 1993)

————, Akosombo Agreement (12 September 1994)

————, Accra Clarification (21 December 1994)

————, Abuja Accord (19 August 1995)

————, Supplement to the Abuja Accord (17 August 1996)

————, ECOWAS Mechanism for Conflict Prevention, Management, Resolution, Peacekeeping and Security, 1999

————, ECOWAS Protocol on Good Governance, 2001.

Ellis, S, *The Mask of Anarchy. The Destruction of Liberia and the Religious Dimension of an African Civil War* (NY: New York University Press, 1999).

Ellis, S, and MacGaffey, J, "Research on Sub-Saharan Africa's Unrecorded International Trade: Some Methodological and Conceptual Problems," *African Studies Review,* 2 (1996).

Evans, G, *Co-operating for Peace* (Camberra: Allen & Unwin, 1994).

Falk, Richard, *Revitalizing International Law* (Ames, Iowa: Iowa State University Press (1989).

Fawcett, L, and Hurrell, A, (ed.), *Regionalism in World Politics. Regional Organization and International Order* (Oxford: Oxford University Press, 1995).

Folsom, R, *European Union Law* (St Paul: West Group, 1999).

Fonteyne, J. P., "The Customary International Law Doctrine of Humanitarian Intervention: Its Current Validity Under the UN Charter," *California Western International Law Journal,* 4 (1974)

Freeman M, "The Philosophical Foundations of Human Rights," *Human Rights Quarterly,* 16 (1994).

Frowein, J, A, "Legal Consequences of International Enforcement in the Case of Security Council Inaction," in J. Delbruck (ed.), *The Future of International Law Enforcement: New Scenarios-New Law?* (Berlin: Duncker & Humblot, 1993).

Furley, O. May, R. (eds.), *Peace Keeping in Africa* (Aldershot: Brookfield, 1998).

Ghanaian Chronicle (Accra), Jan. 17, 2003.

Glennon, M, J., "The New Interventionism: The Search for a Just International Law," *Foreign Affairs,* 78 (1999).

Goldberg, J, "A War Without Purpose in a Country Without Identity," *New York Times Magazine*, January 1995.

Gordenker, L., and Weiss, T, G., (eds.), *NGOs, The UN & Global Governance* (Boulder and London: Lynne Rienner Publishers, 1996).

Gowon, Y, *The Economic Community of West African States: A Study of Political and Economic Integration* Ph.D. thesis, Warwick University

Gray, C, "The Principle of Non-Use of Force," in V. Lowe and C. Warbrick, (eds.), *The United Nations and Principles of International Law: Essays in Memory of Michael Akehurst* (London: Routledge, 1994).

Haas, E. 1993: "Beware the Slippery Slope: Notes Toward the Definition of Justifiable Intervention," In Reed and Kaysen (eds.), *Emerging Norms of Justified Intervention* (Cambridge Mass: American Academy of Arts and Sciences, 1993).

Habernas, J. W. and Rothchild, D, *Africa in World Politics: Post-Cold War Challenges* (Boulder, Colorado: Westview Press).

Haggard, B, and Simmons, B, "Theories of International Regimes," *International Organization*, 41, 3 (1987).

Hashmi, S, "Is There an Islamic Ethic of Humanitarian Intervention?" *Ethics and International Affairs*, 9 (1993).

———, *State Sovereignty: Change and Persistence in International Relations* (Pennsylvania: Pennsylvania State University Press, 1997).

Helton, A. C., "The Legality of Providing Humanitarian Assistance without the Consent of the Sovereign," *International Journal of Refugee Law*, 4 (1992)

Hilaire, Mc. and Justin, M, *Regional Peacekeeping in the Post Cold War Era* (Massachusetts Cambridge: Kluwer law international, 2000).

Hinsley, F, H., *Sovereignty* (New York: Basic Books, 1966).

Hirsch, J, *Sierra Leone: Diamonds and the Struggle for Democracy* (Boulder and London: Lynne Rienner Publishers, 2001).

Hochschild, A, *King Leopold's Ghost: A Story of Greed, Terror, and Heroism in Colonial Africa* (London: Papermac 2000).

Hoffmann, S, *Duties beyond Borders: On the Limits and Possibilities of Ethical International Politics* (Syracuse, NY: Syracuse University Press, 1977).

———, Hoffmann, S, "The Problem of Intervention," in H. Bull *Intervention in World Politics* (Oxford: Clarendon Press, 1984).

———, *The Ethics and Politics of Humanitarian Intervention* (Notre Dame: University Notre Dame Press, 1997).

———, "The Crisis of Liberal Internationalism," *Foreign Policy*, 98 (1995).

———, "The Politics and Ethics of Military Intervention," *Survival* 1995/96.

Holzgrefe, J, L., "The Humanitarian Intervention Debate," in J. L. Holzgrefe and Robert O. Keohane (eds.), *Humanitarian Intervention: ethical, legal and political dilemmas* (Cambridge: Cambridge University Press, 2003).

Howe, H, "Lessons of Liberia: ECOMOG and Regional Peacekeeping," *International Security*, 21 (1996/97).

———, "Private Security Forces and Africa Stability: The Case of Executives Outcomes," *The Journal of Modern African Studies*, 36 (1998).

Hurley, O, *Conflict in Africa* (London: Tauris Academic Studies, 1995).

Hurrell, A, "Explaining the Resurgence of Regionalism in World Politics," *Review of International Studies*, 21 (1995).

————," France: Adjustment to Change," in Hedley Bull (ed.), *The Expansion of International Society* (Oxford: Clarendon Press, 1984).

Hutchful, E, "Peacekeeping Under Conditions of Resource Stringency: Ghana's Army in Liberia," in Jakkie Cilliers and Greg Mills (eds.), *From Peacekeeping to Complex Emergencies: Peace Support Missions in Africa* (Johannesburg and Pretoria: South African Institute of International Affairs, 1999).

Ignatieff, M, *Independent International Commission on Kosovo, Kosovo Report: Conflict, International Response, Lessons Learned* (Oxford: Oxford University Press, 2000).

Ihvonbere, O, and Shaw, C, M., "Hegemonic Participation in Peace-Keeping Operations: The Case of Nigeria and ECOMOG," *International Journal on World Peace* (1996).

International Commission on Intervention and State Sovereignty, *The Responsibility to Protect: Report of the International Commission on Intervention and State Sovereignty* (Ottawa: International Development Research Centre, 2001).

Jackson, R. and Rosberg, C, "The Marginality of the African State," in Patrick O'Meara (ed.), *The First Twenty-Five years* (Bloomington: Indiana University Press, 1986).

————, "Why Africa's Weak States Persist: The Empirical and the Juridical in Statehood," in Atul Kohli (ed.), *The State and Development in the Third World*. Princeton: Princeton University Press, 1986).

————, "Armed Humanitarianism," *International Journal*, 43 (1993).

————, *Quasi States: Sovereignty, International Relations and the Third World* (Cambridge; New York: Cambridge University Press, 1990).

————, "International Community Beyond the Cold War," in Gene M. Lyons and Michael Mastanduno (eds.), *Beyond Westphalia? State Sovereignty and International Intervention* (Baltimore: Johns Hopkins University Press, 1995).

————, *The Global Covenant: Human Conduct in a World of States* (Oxford and New York: Oxford University Press, 2000)

James, A, *Sovereign Statehood: The Basis of International Society* (London: Allen and Unwin, 1986).

Joseph, R, *Democracy and Prebendal Politics in Nigeria: The Rise and Fall of the Second Republic* (New York: Cambridge University Press, 1987).

Kadivar, E, "Ethnopolitical violence in the Liberian civil war," *Journal of Conflict Studies*, (1995).

Kalshoven, F, (ed.), *Assisting the Victims of Armed Conflicts and Other Disasters* (Dordrecht: Nijhoff Publishers, 1989).

Kamenka, E, (ed.), *Human Rights* (London: E. Arnold, 1978).

Kaplan, Robert. "The Coming Anarchy," *Atlantic Monthly*, 1994.

Kelsen, H, *The Law of the United Nations: A Critical Analysis of its Fundamental Problems* (New York: Praeger, 1966).

————, *Principles of International Law* (New York: Rinehart & Company, Inc. 2003). reprint.

Kennan, G, F., "Morality and Foreign Policy," *Foreign Affairs*, 64 (1985/86).

————, *Realities of American Foreign Policy* (Princeton: Princeton University Press, 1954).

Keohane, R, (eds.), *Humanitarian Intervention: Ethical, Legal and Political Dilemmas* (Cambridge: Cambridge University Press, 2003).

————, "Introduction," in Robert O. Keohane and J. L. Holzgrefe, (eds.), *Humanitarian Intervention: Ethical, Legal and Political Dilemmas* (Cambridge: Cambridge University Press, 2003).

Kieh, K, George Jr., "Combatants, Patrons, Peacemakers, and the Liberian Conflict," *Studies in Conflict and Terrorism*, 15 (1992)

Kingsbury, B, "Sovereignty and Inequality," *European Journal of International Law* (1998).

Klaas, V, W, *The Pretence of Peace-keeping: ECOMOG, West Africa and Liberia, 1990–1998* (The Hague: Netherlands Institute of International Relations, 1999).

Kodjoe, O, "Regional Organizations and the Resolution of Internal Conflict: The ECOWAS Intervention in Liberia," *International Peacekeeping*, 1 (1994).

Krasner, S, D., *International Regimes* (Ithaca: Cornell University Press, 1983).

————, "Sovereignty and Intervention" in Gene M. Lyons and Michael Mastanduno (eds.), *Beyond Westphalia? State Sovereignty and International Intervention* (Baltimore: John Hopkins University Press, 1995).

————, *Sovereignty: Organized Hypocrisy* (Princeton: Princeton University Press, 1999).

Kratochwil, F, "Sovereignty as Dominium: Is There a Right to Humanitarian Intervention?" in Gene M. Lyons and Michael Mastanduno (eds.), *Beyond Westphalia? State Sovereignty and International Intervention* (Baltimore: John Hopkins University Press, 1995).

Kufuor, K, "The Legality of ECOWAS Intervention in the Liberian Civil War by the Economic Community of West African States," *African Journal of International and Comparative Law*, 5 (1993).

Kumar, R, "Sovereignty and Intervention: Opinions in South Asia," *Pugwash Occasional Papers* (2001).

Kuper, L, *Genocide: Its Use in the Twentieth Century* (New Haven: Yale University Press, 1982).

Lancaster, C, "The Lagos Three: Economic Regionalism in Sub-Saharan Africa," in John Harbeson and Donald Rothchild, (eds.), *Africa in World Politics*, 2nd edn. (Boulder: Westview, 1995).

Lepard, B, *Rethinking Humanitarian Intervention: A Fresh Legal Approach based on Fundamental Ethical Principles in International Law and World Religions* (Pennsylvania: Pennsylvania State University Press, 2002)

Levitt, J, "Humanitarian Intervention by Regional Actors in Internal Conflicts: The Cases of ECOWAS in Liberia and Sierra Leone," *Temple International and Comparative Law Journal* (1998).

Liebenow, J, G, *Liberia: The Evolution of Privilege* (Ithaca, NY.: Cornell University Press, 1969).

————, *Liberia: The Quest for Democracy* (Bloomington: Indiana University Press, 1987).

Lillich R, B., "Humanitarian Intervention: A Reply to Ian Brownlie and a Plea for Constructive Alternatives," in John Norton Moore (ed.), *Law and Civil War in the Modern World* (Baltimore: John Hopkins University Press, 1974).

———, "Kant and the Current Debate over Humanitarian Intervention," *Journal of Transnational Law and Policy,* (1997).

Lin Y, *My Country, My People* (New York: The John Day Company, 1939).

Little, R, *Intervention: External Involvement in Internal Wars* (NJ: Rowman and Littlefield, 1995).

Lowe, V, "The Principle of Non-intervention: The Use of Force," in Vaughan Lowe and Colin Warbrick (eds.), *The United Nations and the Principles of International Law: Essays in Memory of Michael Akehurst* (London: Routledge, 1994)

Lowenkopt, M, "Liberia: Putting the State Back Together," in I. Zartman (ed.), *Collapsed States: The Disintegration and Restoration of Legitimate Authority* (Boulder, Col.: Lynne Reinner, 1995).

Luttwak, E, N., "Kofi's Rule: Humanitarian Intervention and Neocolonialism," *The National Interest 58,* (2000).

Lyons, G, *Beyond Westphalia* (Baltimore: The Johns Hopkings University Press, 1995).

Lyons, T, *Voting For Peace: Post Conflict Elections in Liberia* (Washington, DC: The Brookings Institution, 1999).

Magyar, K, and Morgan, E, *Peacekeeping in Africa: ECOMOG in Liberia* (NY: St. Martin's Press, INC, 1998).

Makinda, S, M., *Seeking Peace from Chaos: Humanitarian Intervention in Somalia* (Boulder: Colo.: Lynne Rienner, 1993).

Malanczuk, P, *Humanitarian Intervention and the Legitimacy of the Use of Force* (Amsterdam: Het Spinhuis, 1994).

———, *Akehurst's Modern Introduction to International Law,* 7th edn. (London and New York: Routledge, 1997).

Mandelbaum, Micheal, "The Reluctance to Intervene," *Foreign Policy* Summer (1994)

Mansfield, E, "Democratization and the Danger of War," *International Security* 20 (1995).

March, J, G., and Olsen J, P., *Democratic Governance* (New York: The Free Press, 1995).

Martin, G, "Continuity and Change in Franco African Relations," *Journal of Modern African Studies* 33 (1995).

Mason, A, and Wheeler, N, "Realist Objections to Humanitarian Intervention," in Barry Holden (ed.), *The Ethical Dimension of Global Change* (Basingstoke: Macmillan Press, 1996).

McCoubrey, H. and White N, *International Organizations and Civil Wars* (Aldershot: Dartmouth, 1995).

McGarry, J. and O'Leary, B. (eds.), *The Politics of Ethnic Conflict Regulation.* (London: Routledge, 1995).

Migdal, J, *Strong Societies and Weak States: State-Society Relations and State Capabilities in the Third World* (Princeton: NJ: Princeton University Press, 1988).

———, (ed.), *State Power and Social Forces: Domination and Transformation in the Third World* (Cambridge; N.Y: Cambridge University Press, 1994).

Mill, J, S., *On Liberty* (Indianapolis: Bobbs-Merill, 1956).

Moore, D, *Humanitarian Agendas, State Reconstruction and Democratisation Processes in War-torn Societies* (Geneva: United Nations High Commissioner for Refugees, 2000).

Moore, J, *Hard Choices: Moral Dilemmas in Humanitarian Intervention* (New York: Rowman Littlefield, 1998).

Morgenthau, H, *Politics Among Nations* (New York: Alfred A. Knopf, 1954).

Mortimer, Robert, "From ECOMOG to ECOMOG II: Intervention in Sierra Leone," in John W. Harbeson and Donald Rothchild (eds.), *Africa in World Politics: The African State System in Flux*, 3rd edn, (Boulder and Oxford Westview Press, 2000).

———, "Sénégal's Role in ECOMOG: The Francophone Dimension," *Journal of Modern African Studies*, 34 (1996).

Murphy, S, D., *Humanitarian Intervention: The United Nations in an Evolving World Order* (Philadelphia: University of Pennsylvania Press, 1996).

Nardin, T. and Mapel, D. (eds.) *Traditions of International Ethics* (Cambridge: Cambridge University Press, 1992).

———, "The Moral Basis of Humanitarian Intervention," *Ethics and International Affairs* 16, (2002).

Nass, I. A, *A Study in Internal Conflicts: The Liberian Crisis & The West African Initiative* (Emugu, Nigeria: Fourth Dimension Publishing, 2000).

Nelson, H, D., *Liberia: A Country Study* (Washington, DC: American University, 1984).

Nolan, C, J., *Greenwood Encyclopedia of International Relations* (Westport, CT: Greenwood Pub., 2002).

Nowrot, K, and Shabacker, E, W., "The Use of Force to Restore Democracy: International Legal Implications of the ECOWAS Intervention in Sierra Leone," *American University International Law Review*, 14 (1998).

Ofodile, A, C., "The Legality of ECOWAS Intervention in Liberia," *Columbia Journal of Transnational Law*, 32, (1994).

Ofuatey, K, W., "Regional Organizations and the Resolution of Internal Conflict: The ECOWAS intervention in Liberia," *International Peacekeeping*, 1/3 (1994).

Okukotun, A, "Authoritarian State, Crisis of Democratization and the Underground Media in Nigeria," *African Affairs*, (2002).

Olonisakin, F, "Africa Home-Made Peacekeeping Initiatives," *Armed Forces and Society*, 23/3 (1997).

———, *Reinventing Peacekeeping in Africa: Conceptual and Legal Issues In ECOMOG Operations* (London: Kluwer Law International, 2000).

Onuf, N, "Intervention for the Common Good," in Gene M. Lyons and Michael Mastanduno, (eds.), *Beyond Westphalia? State Sovereignty and International Intervention* (Baltimore: Johns Hopkins University Press, 1995).

———, "Sovereignty: Outline of a Conceptual History," *Alternatives* 16 (1991).

Pakenham, T, *The Scramble for Africa 1876–1912* (London: Weidenfeld & Nicolson, 1991).

Paris, R, "Peacebuilding and the Limits of Liberal Internationalism," *International Security* (1997).

Pease K., and Forsythe, D, P., "Human Rights, Humanitarian Intervention, and World Politics," *Human Rights Quarterly*, 15 (1993).

Pellet, A, "State Sovereignty and the Protection of Fundamental Human Rights: An International Law Perspective," in *Pugwash Occasional Papers* 1 (2000).

Petersen, F, J., "The Façade of Humanitarian Intervention for Human Rights in a Community of Sovereign Nations," *Arizona Journal of International and comparative Law,* 15 (1998).

Philips, R, L. and Cady, D, L. (eds.), "The Ethics of Humanitarian Intervention," *Humanitarian Intervention: Just War vs. Pacifism* (London: Rowman&Littlefield, (1996).

Pollis A, and Shawb, P, eds., *Human Rights Cultural and Ideological Perspectives* (New York: Praeger Publishers, 1979).

Ramsbotham, O, "Humanitarian Intervention 1990–1995: A Need to Reconceptualize?" *Review of International Studies,* 23 (1999).

Ramsbotham, O, and Woodhouse, T, (eds.), *Humanitarian Intervention in Contemporary Conflict: A Reconceptualization* (Cambridge: Polity Press, 1996).

Rawls, J, *The Law of Peoples* (Cambridge: Harvard University Press, 1999).

Reisman, W, M., "Sovereignty and Human Rights in Contemporary International Law," *American Journal of International Law,* 84 (1990).

———, "Humanitarian Intervention and Fledgling Democracies," *Fordham International Law Journal,* 18 (1995).

———, "Humanitarian Intervention to Protect the Ibos," in Richard Lillich (ed.), *Humanitarian Intervention and the United Nations* (Charlottesville: University Press of Virginia, 1973).

Reno, William, "The Business of War in Liberia," *Current History,* 95 (1996)

———, *Warlords Politics and African States* (Boulder and London: Lynne Rienner, 1998).

Richards, Paul, *Fighting for the Rain Forest: War, Youth, and Resources in Sierra Leone.* (Oxford: James Currey, 1998).

Rich, B, "Warlords, State Fragmentation and Dilemma of Humanitarian Intervention," *Small Wars and Insurgencies,* 10 (1999).

Rideau, Joël, *Le Droit Des Communautés Européennes* (Paris : Presses Universitaires De France, 1995).

Riggs, F, "The Nation State and Other Actors," in James Rosenau, *International Politics and Foreign Policy* (New York, The Free Press, 1969).

Rivilin, B, "Regional Arrangements and The UN System for Security and Conflict Resolution," *International Relations,* 11 (1992).

Roberts, A, "Humanitarian War: Military Intervention and Human Rights," *International Affairs,* 69 (1993).

———, The So-called 'Right' of Humanitarian Intervention" *Yearbook of International Humanitarian Law,* 3 (2000).

———, "A New age in International Relations?" *International Affairs,* 67 (1991).

Robson, P, *Integration, Development and Equity: Economic Integration in West Africa* (London: George Allen & Unwin, 1983).

Rosenau, J, "Intervention as a Scientific Concept," *Journal of Conflict Resolution,* 1 (1969).

———, "The Concept of Intervention," *Journal of International Affairs,* 2 (1968).

Rotberg, R, I., "Africa's Mess, Mugabe's Mayhem," *Foreign Affairs* (2000).

Rufin, J, C., *Le piége humanitaire* (Paris: Claude Lattés, 1986)

Ruiz H, *Uprooted Liberians: Casualties of a Brutal War* (Washington, DC: US Committee for Refugees, 1992).

Rupesinghe, K, *Internal Conflict and Governance* (London: Macmillan, 1992).

Schachter, O, "The legality of pro-democratic invasion," *American Journal of International Law*, 78 (1984).

Scheffer, D, J., "Towards a Modern Doctrine of Humanitarian Intervention," *University of Toledo Law Review*, 23 (1992).

Sesay, M, A., "Collective Security or Collective Disaster?" *Security Dialogue*, 26 (1995).

Shklar, Judith, *Legalism* (Cambridge, Massachusetts: Harvard University Press, 1964).

Shulong, C, "China, Asia and Issue of Intervention and Sovereignty," *Pugwash Occasional Papers*, 2 (2001).

Simma, B, "NATO, the UN and the Use of Force: Legal Aspects," *European Journal of International Law*, 10 (1999).

———, (ed.), *The Charter of the United Nations: A Commentary* (Oxford and New York: Oxford University Press, 2002).

Simon, D, "The State and Human Rights: Sovereignty versus Humanitarian Intervention," *International Relations* 12 (1994).

Skocpol, T, "Bringing the State Back In: Strategies of analysis in Current Research," in Peter Evans, Dietrich Rueschemeyer, and Theda Skocpol (ed.), *Bringing the State Back In* (Cambridge, New York: Cambridge University Press, 1985).

Slater, Jerome and Nardin, Terry "Non-Iintervention and Human Rights," *Journal of Politics*, (1986)

Smith, M, "Humanitarian Intervention: An Overview of Ethical Issues," *Ethics and International Affairs*, 12 (1998).

Smith, C, V., A, *Light Weapons Proliferation in Southern Africa* (London: Center for Defense 1997).

Smouts, M-C, *Les Nouvelles Relations Internationales* (Paris: Presses de Sciences PO, 1998).

Song, L, B., "The New International Law: Protection of Rights of Individuals rather Than of States," *American Journal of International Law Review* (1982).

Stiglitz, E. J, *Globalization and its Discontents* (New York: Norton, 2002).

Stremlau, J, *The International Politics of the Nigerian Civil War, 1967–1970* (Princeton: Princeton University Press, 1977).

Tesòn, F, R., *Humanitarian Intervention: An Inquiry into Law and Morality* (2nd edn, Irvington-on-Hudson: Transnational Publishers, 1997).

———, "Kantian International Liberalism," in David R. Mapel and Terry Nardin (eds.), *International Society: Diverse Ethical Perspectives* (Princeton: Princeton University Press, 1998).

———, *A Philosophy of International Law* (Boulder: Westview Press, 1998).

———, "The liberal case for humanitarian intervention," in J. L. Holzgrefe and Robert O. Keohane (eds.), *Humanitarian Intervention: Ethical, Legal, and Political Dilemmas* (Cambridge: Cambridge University Press, 2003).

United Nations, Security Council Resolutions:
———, UN Document S/RES/788 (1992). 19 November 1992.
———, UN Document S/RES/813. 26 March 1993.
———, UN Document S/RES/856. 10 August 1993.
———, UN Document S/RES/866. 22 September 1993.
———, UN Document S/RES/911. 21 April 1994.
———, UN Document S/RES/950. 21 October 1994
———, UN Document S/RES/972. 13 January 1995
———, UN Document S/RES/985. 13 April 1995.
———, UN Document S/RES/1001. 30 June 1995
———, UN Document S/RES/1014. 15 September 1995.
———, UN Document S/RES/1020. 10 November 1995.
———, UN Document S/RES/1041. 29 January 1996.
———, UN Document S/RES/1059. 31 May 1996
———, UN Document S/RES/1071. 30 August 1996.
———, UN Document S/RES/1083. 27 November 1996.
———, UN Document S/RES/1100. 27 March 1997.
———, UN Document S/RES/1116. 27 June 1997.
United Nations, Presidential Statements of the Security Council.
———, S/22133 (22 January 1991)
———, S23886 (7 May 1992)
———, S/25918 (June 1993)
United Nations Reports of the Secretary General
———, on the Question of Liberia S/25402. 12 March 1993.
———, Twenty-Second Progress Report of the Secretary General on the UN
    Observer Mission in Liberia. S/1997/237. 19 March 1997.
———, Final Report of the Secretary General in Liberia. S/1997/237. 12 September
    1997. 12 September 1997. 19 March 1997.
———, "The causes of conflicts and the promotion of durable peace and sustain-
    able development in Africa," Report of the Secretary General A/52/871-
    S/1998/318
———, Report of the Inter-Agency Mission to West Africa, "Towards a Compre-
    hensive Approach to Durable and Sustainable Solutions to Priority Needs and
    Challenges in West Africa," UN Security Council document, S2001/434, 2
    May 2001.
Vales, H, "The Latin American View on the Doctrine of Humanitarian Intervention,"
    Journal of Humanitarian Assistance http://www.Jha.ac/articles/ (May 2001).
Vattel, de Emmerick, *Le Droit des Gens ou Principe de la Loi Naturelle* (London:
    1758).
Vogt, M, (ed.), *The Liberian Crisis and ECOMOG: A Bold Attempt at Regional
    Peacekeeping* (Lagos: Gabumo Press, 1993).
Vincent, R. J., "Grotius, Human Rights and Intervention," in Hedley Bull, Benedict
    Kingsbury, and Adam Roberts (eds.), *Hugo Grotius and International Rela-
    tions* (Oxford: Clarendon Press, 1990).
———, *Non-intervention and International Order* (Princeton: Princeton University
    Press, 1974).

————, *Human Rights and International Relations* (Cambridge: Cambridge University Press, 1986).

Walle, V, D., "Neopatrimonial Regimes and Political Transitions in Africa," *World Politics,* vol. 46, no. 4 (1994).

Walzer, M, *Just and Unjust Wars: A Moral Argument with Historical Illustrations* 3rd edn. (New York: Basic Books, 2000).

————, "The Moral Standing of States: A Response to Four Critics," *Philosophy and Public Affairs,* 9 (1980).

Weber, M, "The Fundamental Concepts of Sociology," in Talcott Parsons, (ed.), *The Theory of Social and Economic Organization* (New York: Free Press, 1964).

Weiss, T, *The United Nations and Changing World Politics* (Boulder: Westview Press, 1997).

Weller, M, (ed.), *Regional Peace-Keeping and International Enforcement: The Liberian Crisis* (Cambridge: Cambridge University Press, 1994)

West Africa Magazine, 1990

————, 1980

————, 1993

————, 1995

————, 1997

Wheeler, N, *Saving Strangers* (Oxford and New York, Oxford University Press, 2000).

————, "Pluralist or Solidarist Conceptions of International Society: Bull and Vincent on Humanitarian Intervention," *Millennium,* 21 (1992).

Wippman, D, "Enforcing the Peace: ECOWAS and the Liberian Civil War," in Lori Fisler Damrosch ed., *Enforcing Restraint: Collective Intervention in Internal Conflicts* (New York: Council on Foreign Relations, 1993).

World Bank, *Sub-Saharan Africa: From Crisis to Sustainable Growth* (Washington, D.C: The World Bank Group Publications, 2003).

Zakaria, F, "The Rise of Illiberal Democracy," *Foreign Affairs,* 76 (1996).

Zartman, William I. (ed.). *Collapsed States: The Disintegration and Restoration of Legitimate Authority* (Boulder, CO: Lynne Rienner Publishers, 1995).

Index